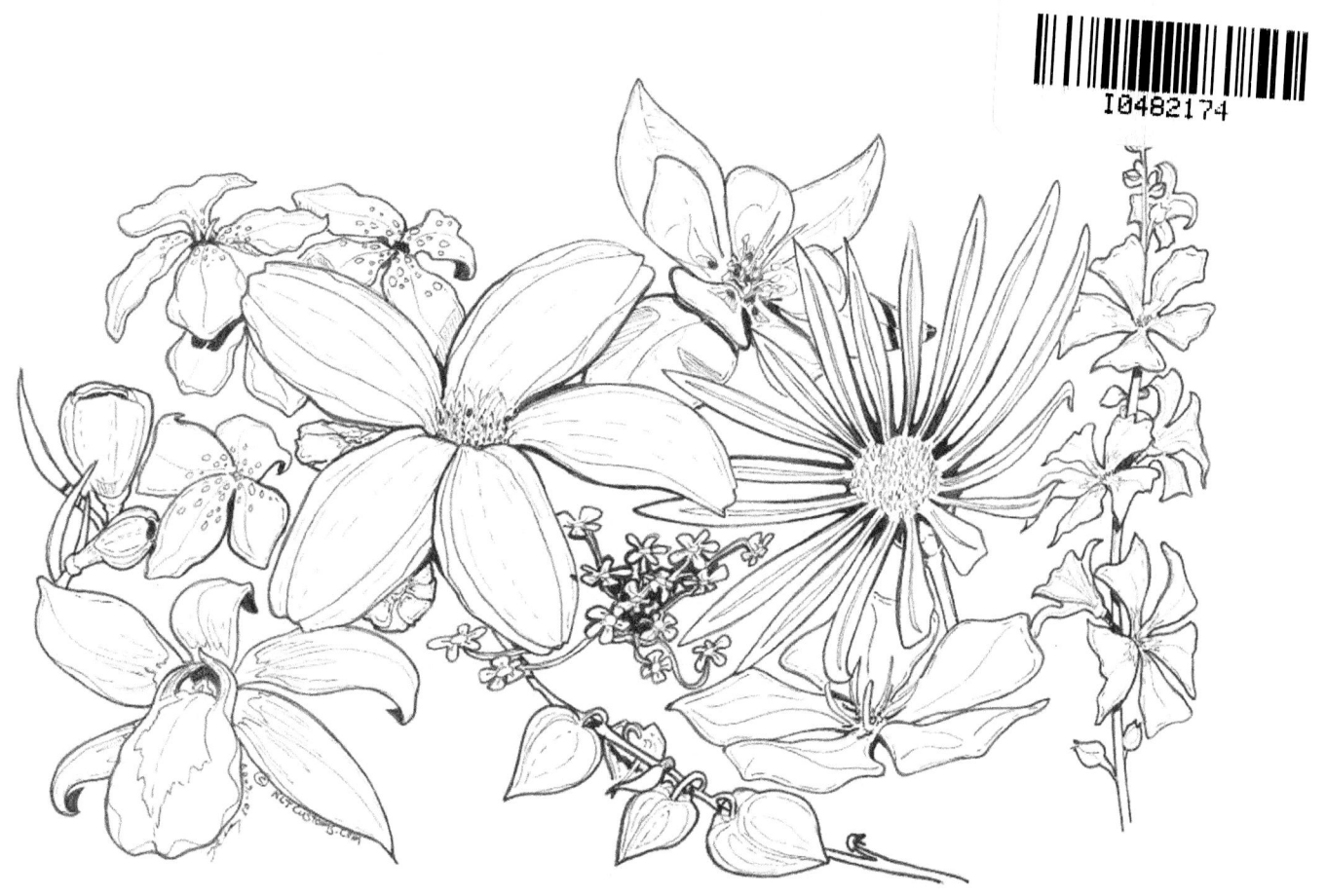

Floral Fantasy
COLORING BOOK

— ILLUSTRATED BY —
Kent L. Talley

Illustrations by
Kent L. Talley

Published by
R&R Publishing
11805 Sylvester Drive
Oklahoma City, OK 73162-1018
(405) 822-8300
www.drtalley.com

Second Edition & Style Updates by
Phillip Grimes
The Creative Guy

First Edition Layout by
Paula Corley
Jot and Tittle Editing

Anthurium

Also called Tailflower or Flamingo Flower.
They are often used indoor because
of their air filtering properties.

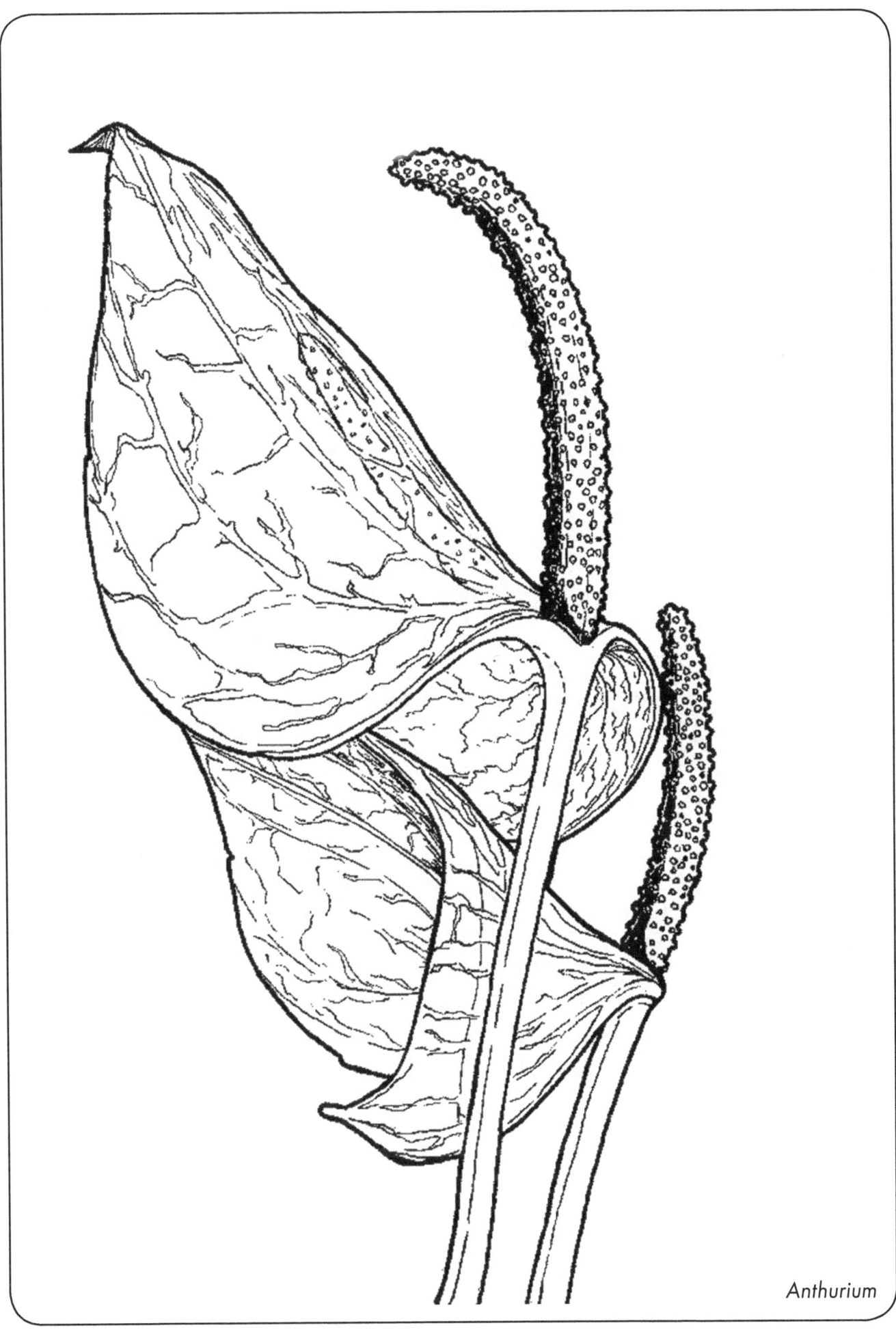

Anthurium

Lillies

Lillies, or the Lilium family is found in many countries around the world.
They come in all the colors of the rainbow and then some.
The patterns on the petals differ from plant to plant.

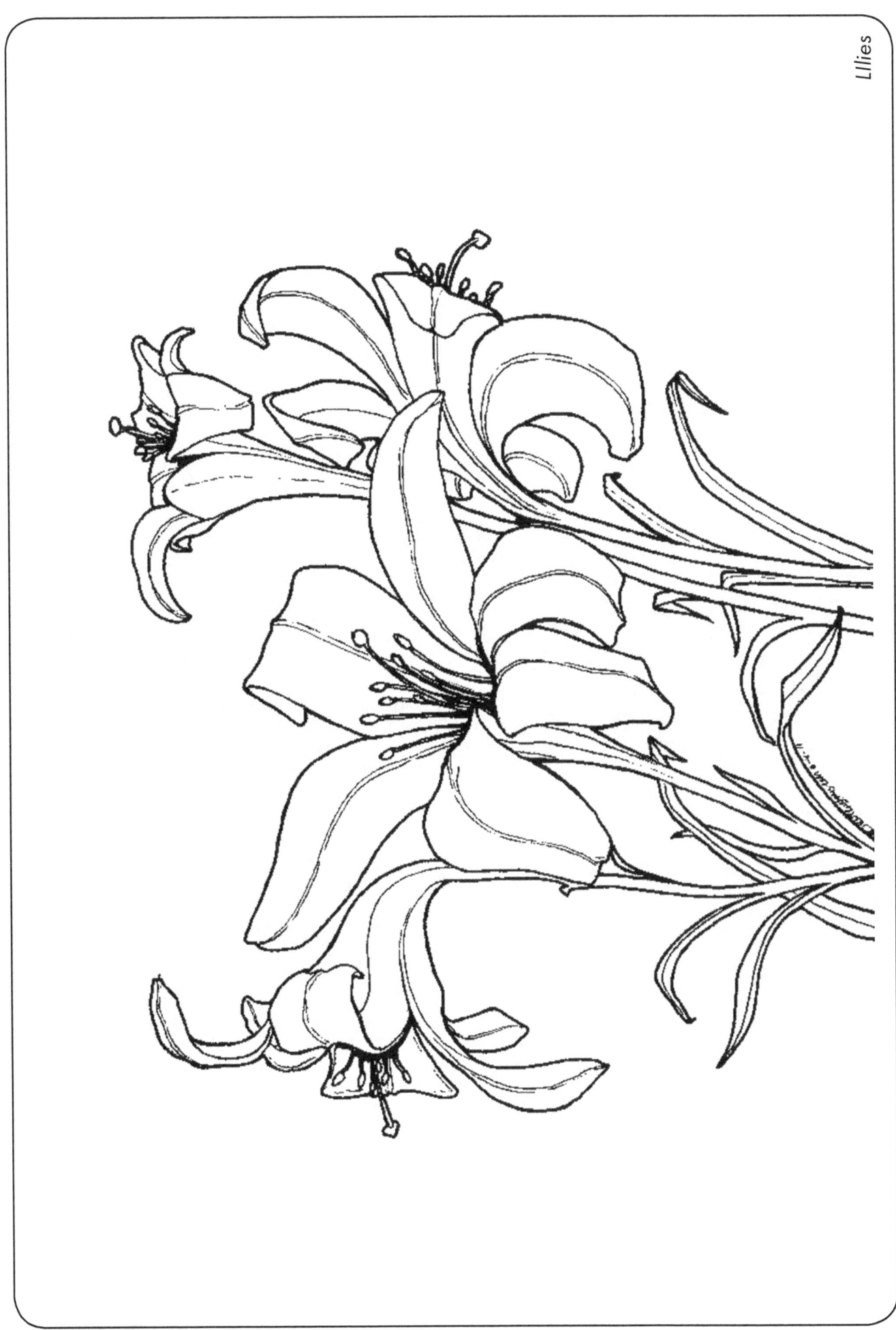

Bouquet

A bouquet is a creative arrangement of flowers.
Bouquets are often arranged in decorative vases or planters.
Some of the first known flower bouquets go as far back as 2500 BC.

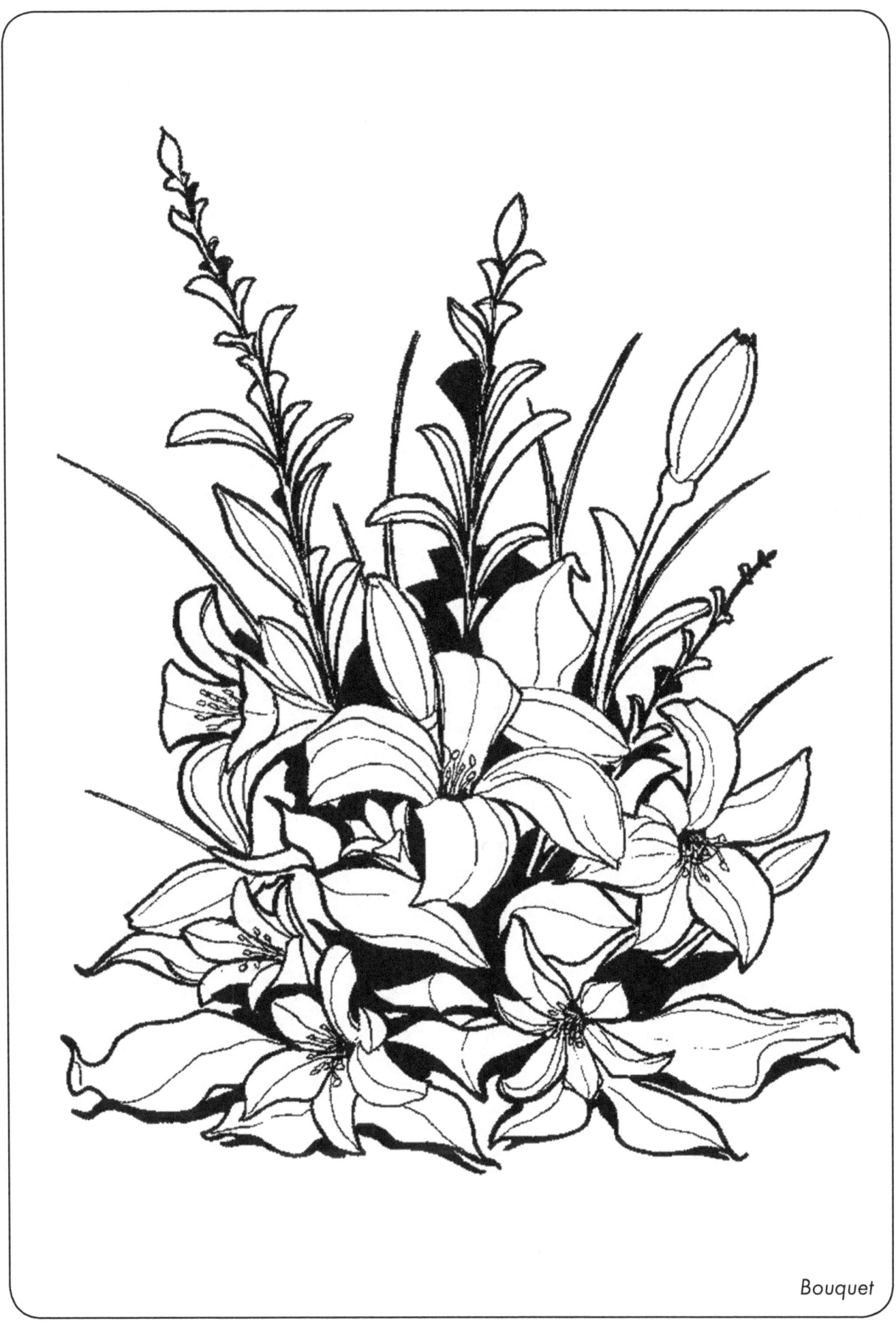

Bouquet

Echinocereus Poselgeri

Also known as Dahlia Cactus, the Echinocereus Poselgeri is native to Southern Texas. Echinocereus Poselgeri has bright pink flowers.

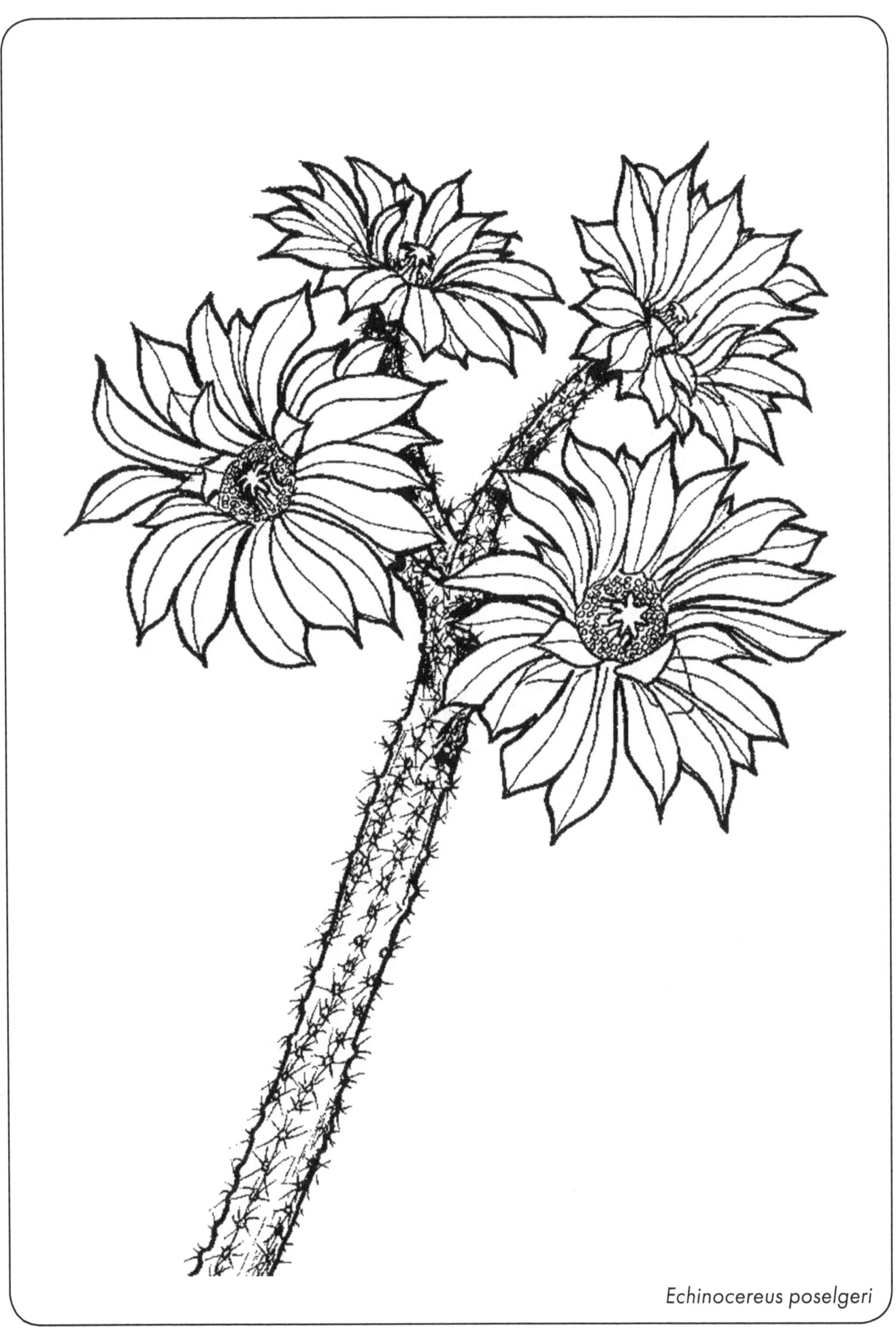

Echinocereus poselgeri

Grapes

Grapes are a very useful and tasty fruit.
This vined berry was cultivated for over 8,000 years
in what is now the Middle East.

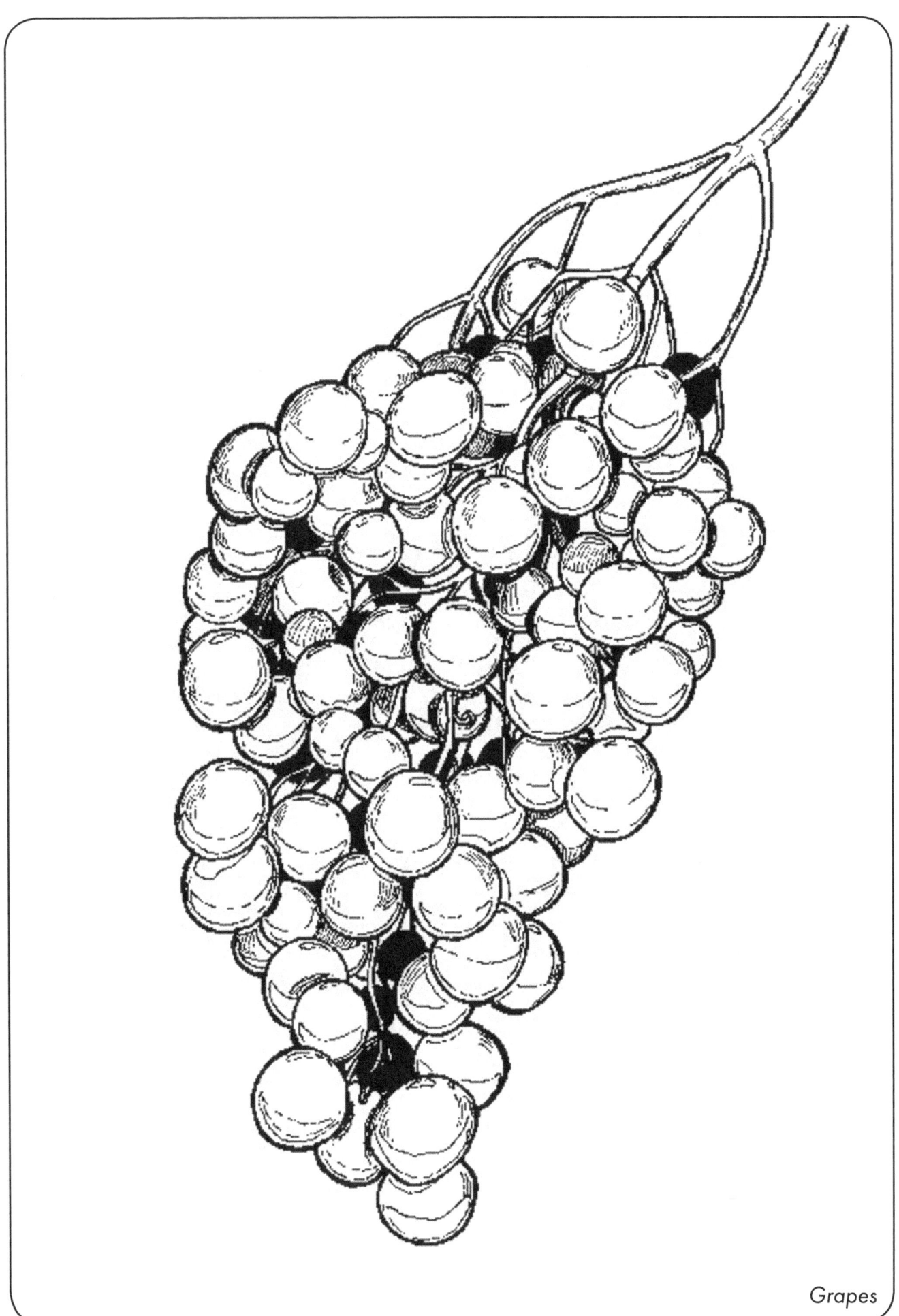

Grapes

Roses

Roses come in several colors and sizes.
In fact, there are over one hundred different species.
Roses are a woody perennial flowering plant.

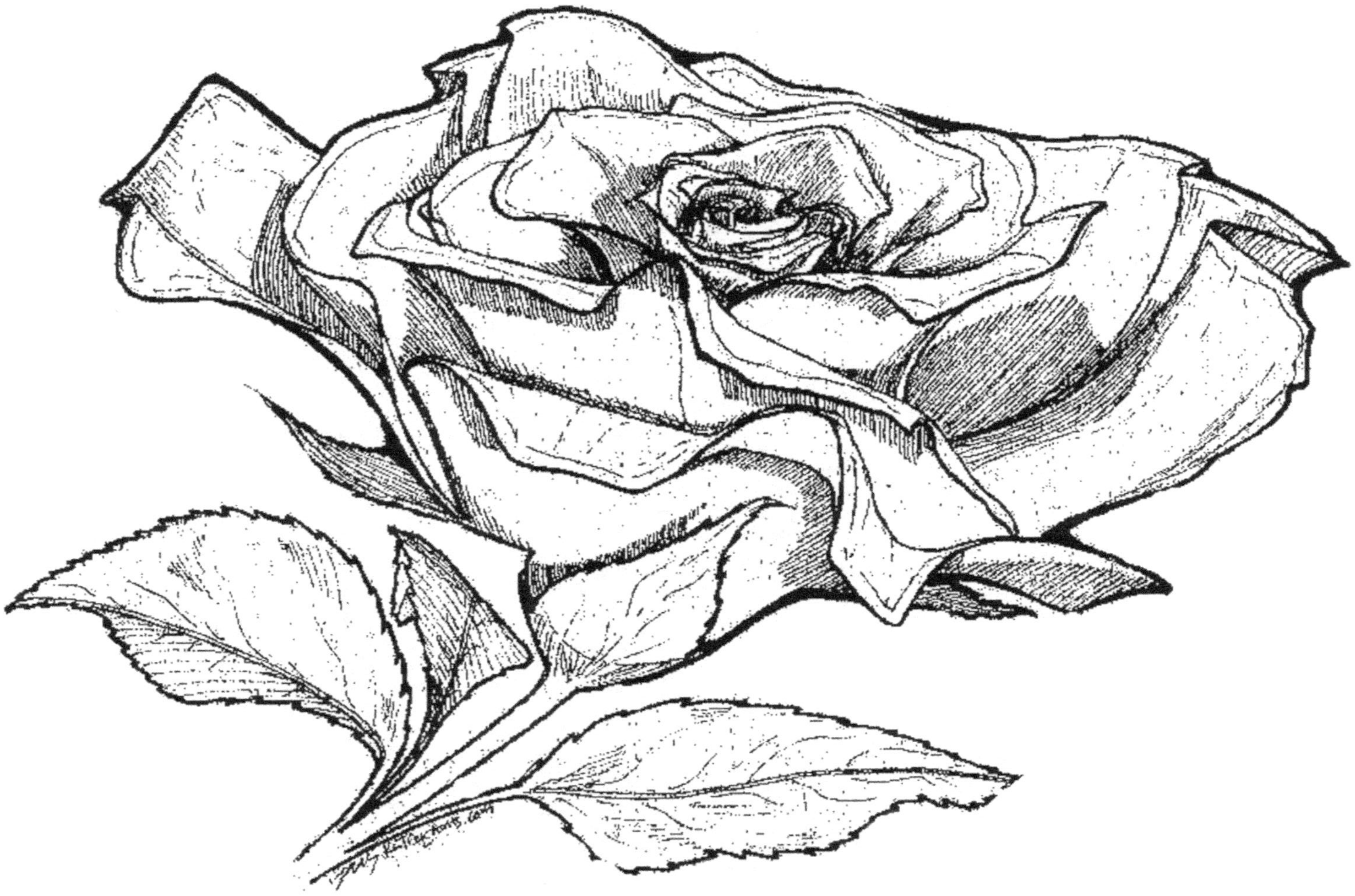

Rose

Hydrangeas

There are over 700 different species of Hydrangeas.
The majority of Hydrangeas species are found in Asia,
though some can be found natively in the Americas.

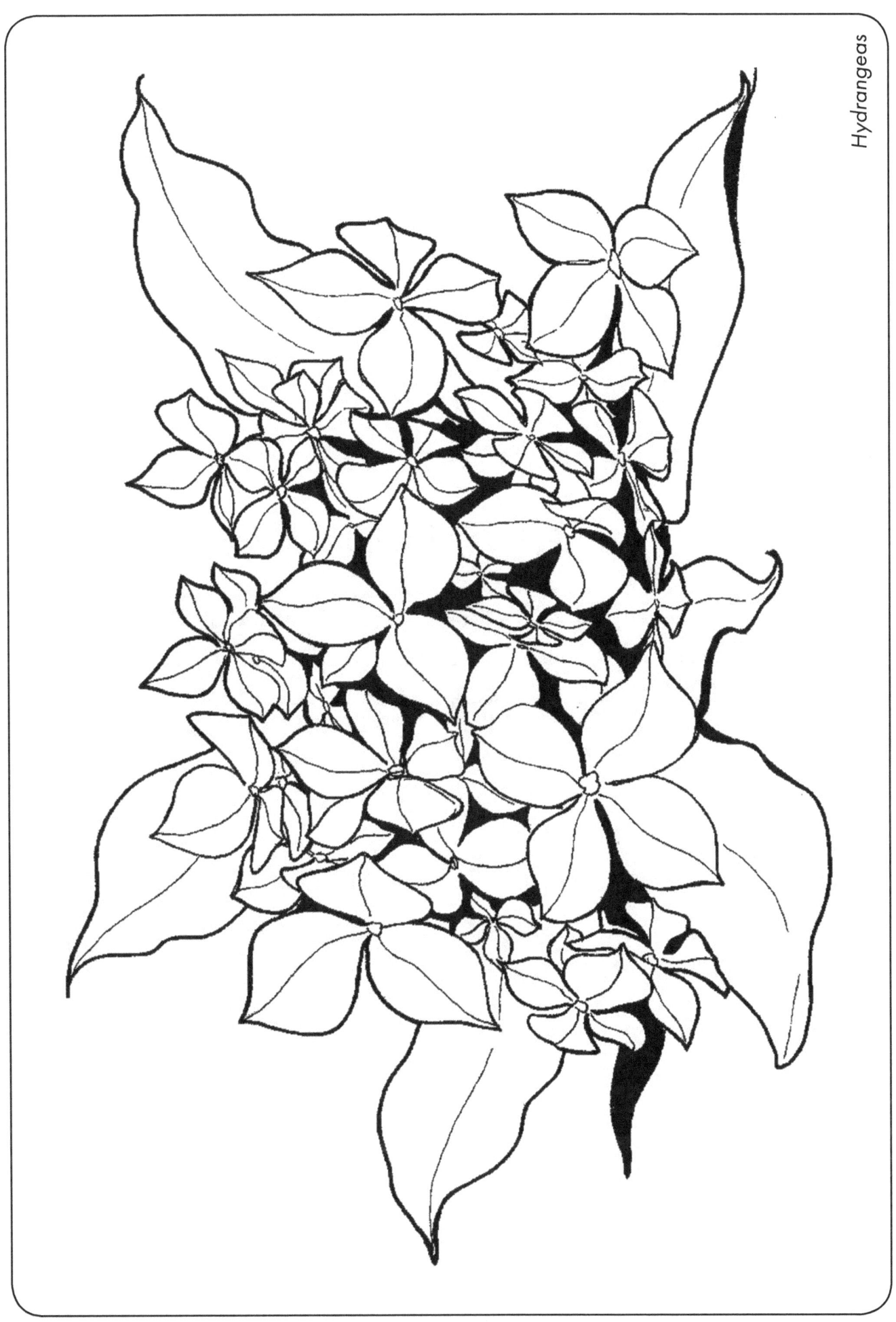

Calla Lilies

Calla Lilies are a trumpet-looking foliage that start to bloom
in mid to late summer. The blooming can last for weeks.
They come in several colors and sizes.

Calla lilies

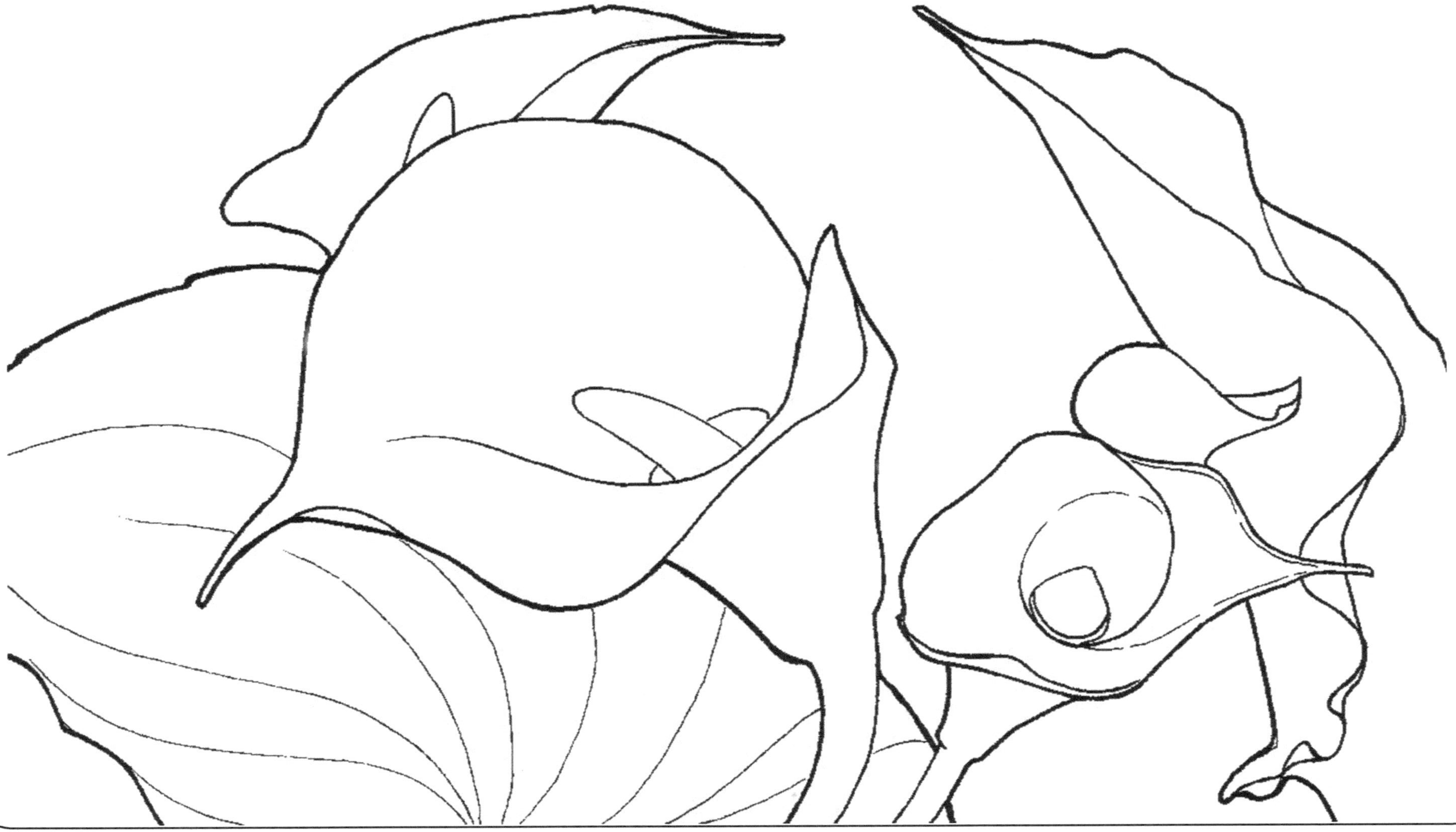

Poppies

Poppy flowers are an ancient plant prized by gardeners for their wide variety
of colors and double blooms in the cooler seasons.
Poppies are know to grow on battle-scared earth.
White poppies symbolize death and rebirth.
The red represents fallen soldiers on Veterans Day in the United States.

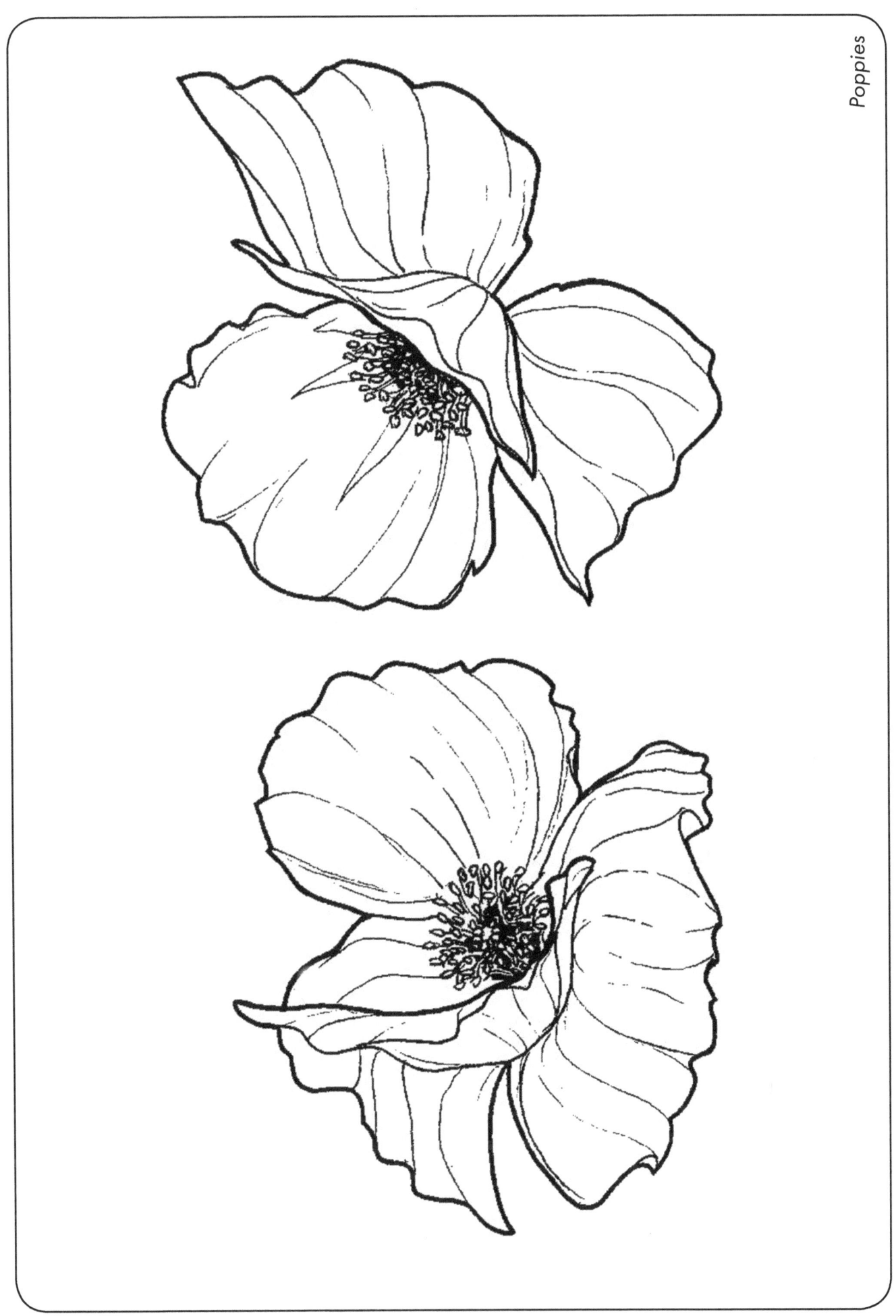

Lotus

The ancient Lotus flower is native to India and Vietnam. The amazing colors
and petal designs of these flowers can be seen blooming in
clean river water just off the muddy shoreline.

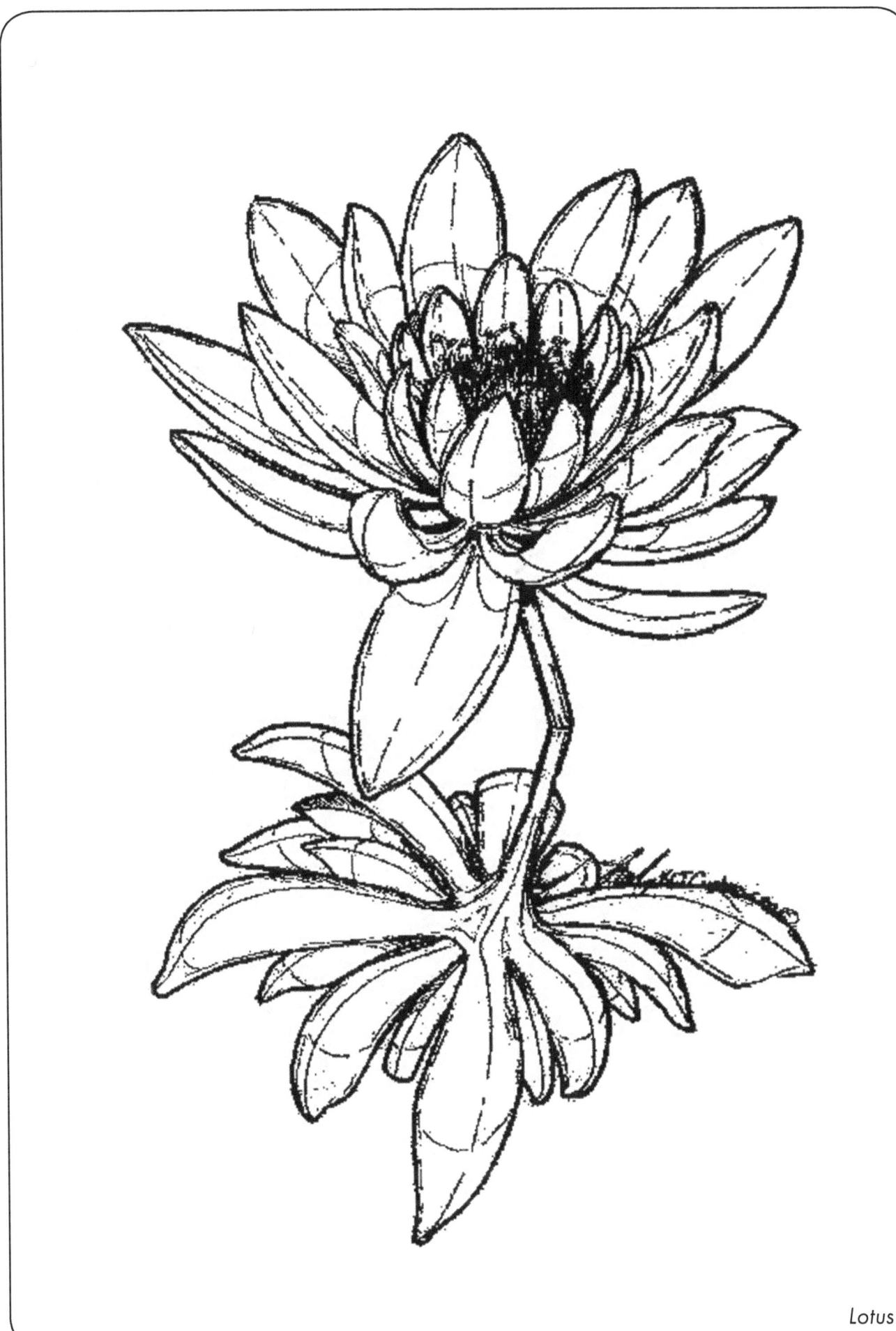

Lotus

Bouquet

Flower arranging was an art form brought to Japan by Buddhist monks.
The Dutch started using floral arrangements as an art form
in the 18th century to decorate homes both inside and out.

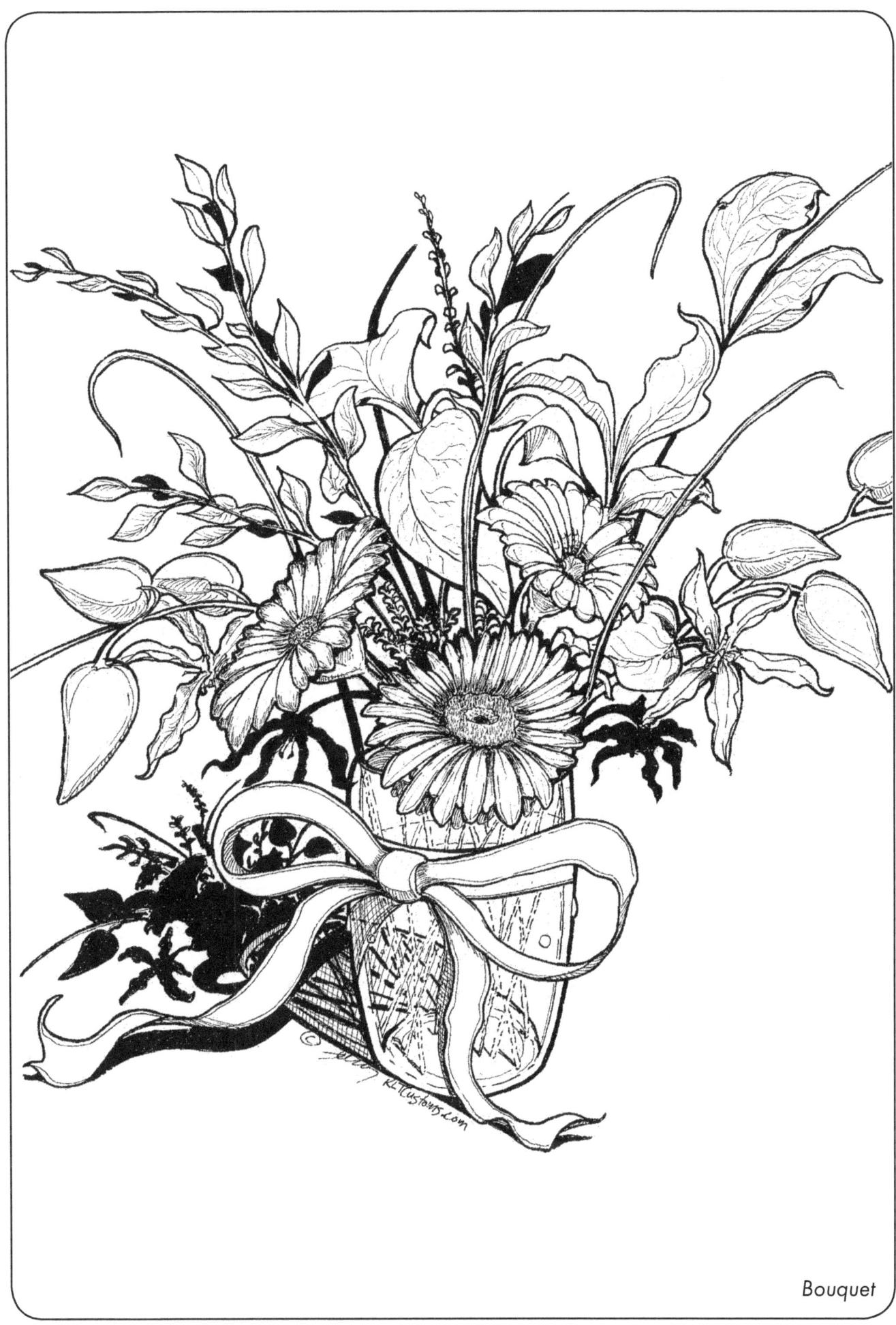

Bouquet

Greenhouse Glory

Garden with watermelon, cantaloupe, bell peppers, cucumbers, squash, tomatoes, peas, and pumpkins.

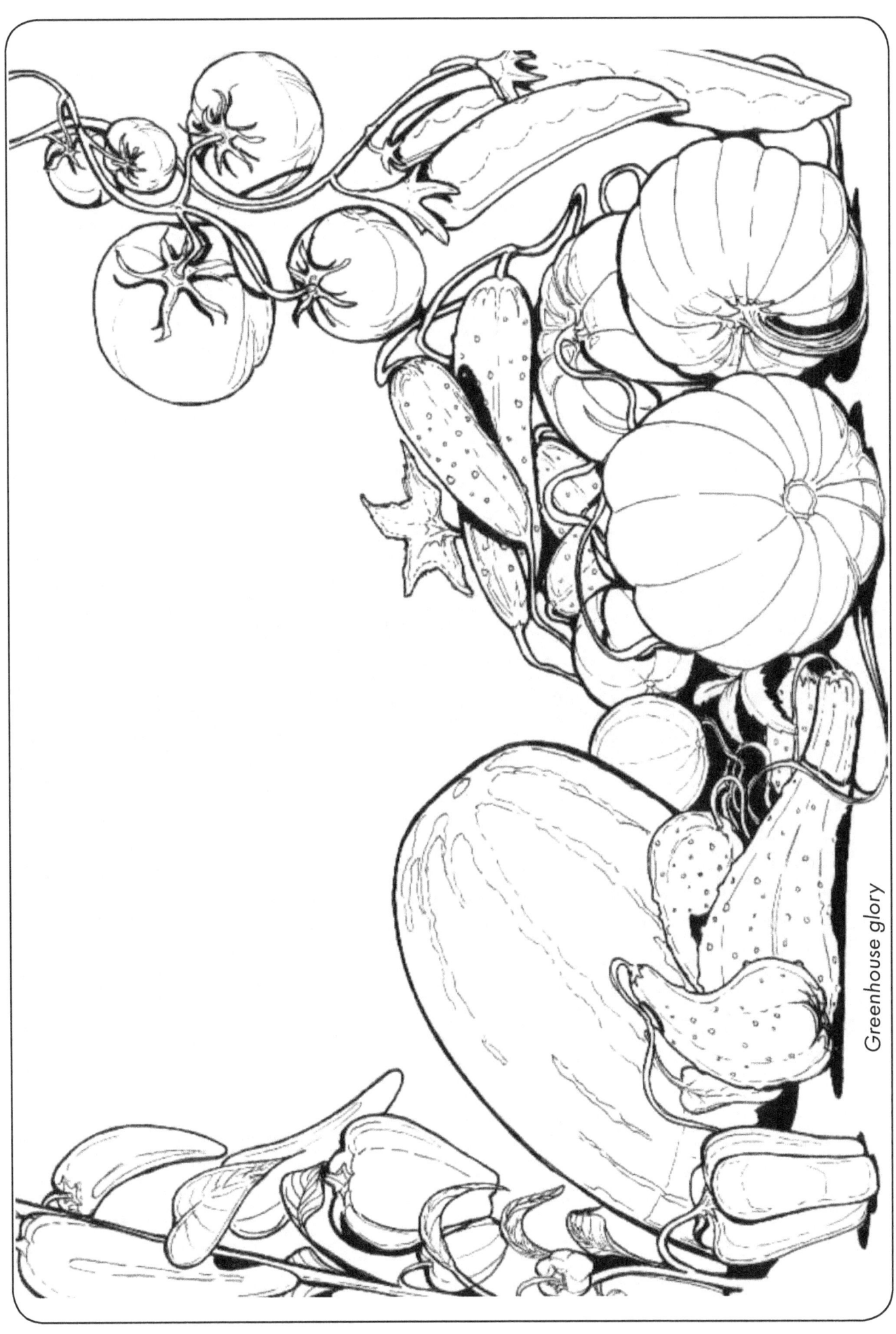

Greenhouse glory

Iris

The Bearded Iris is a very easy plant to maintain.
Once you plant them, pencil thin buds spring up.
If they are taken care of, Irises can come back every year.

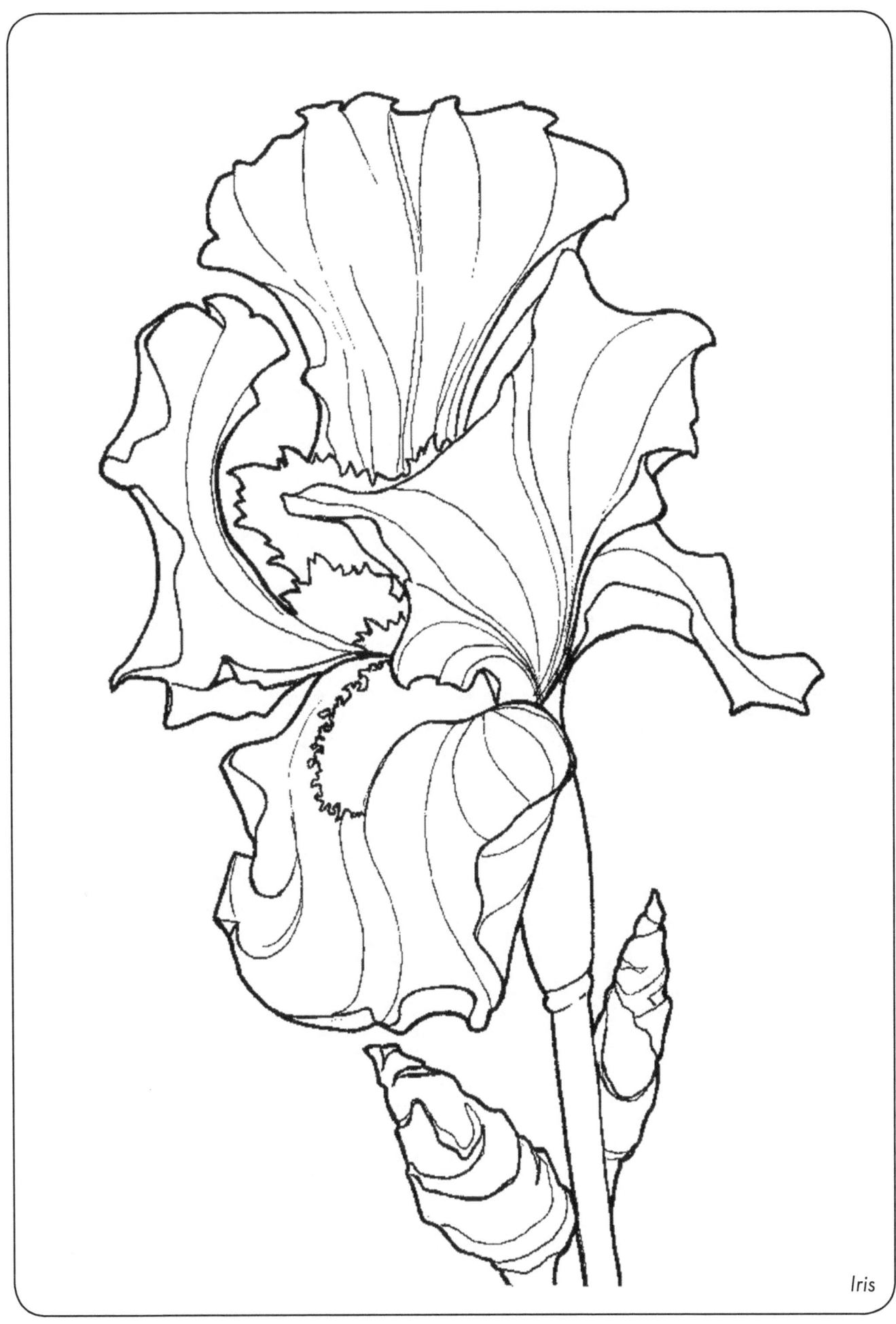

Iris

Maple Leaf

The majestic Maple Leaf is a symbol of Canada and is featured on the Canadian flag. These leaves have a wonderful green color in the summer and shift to beautiful, deep shades of red, orange and yellow in the fall.

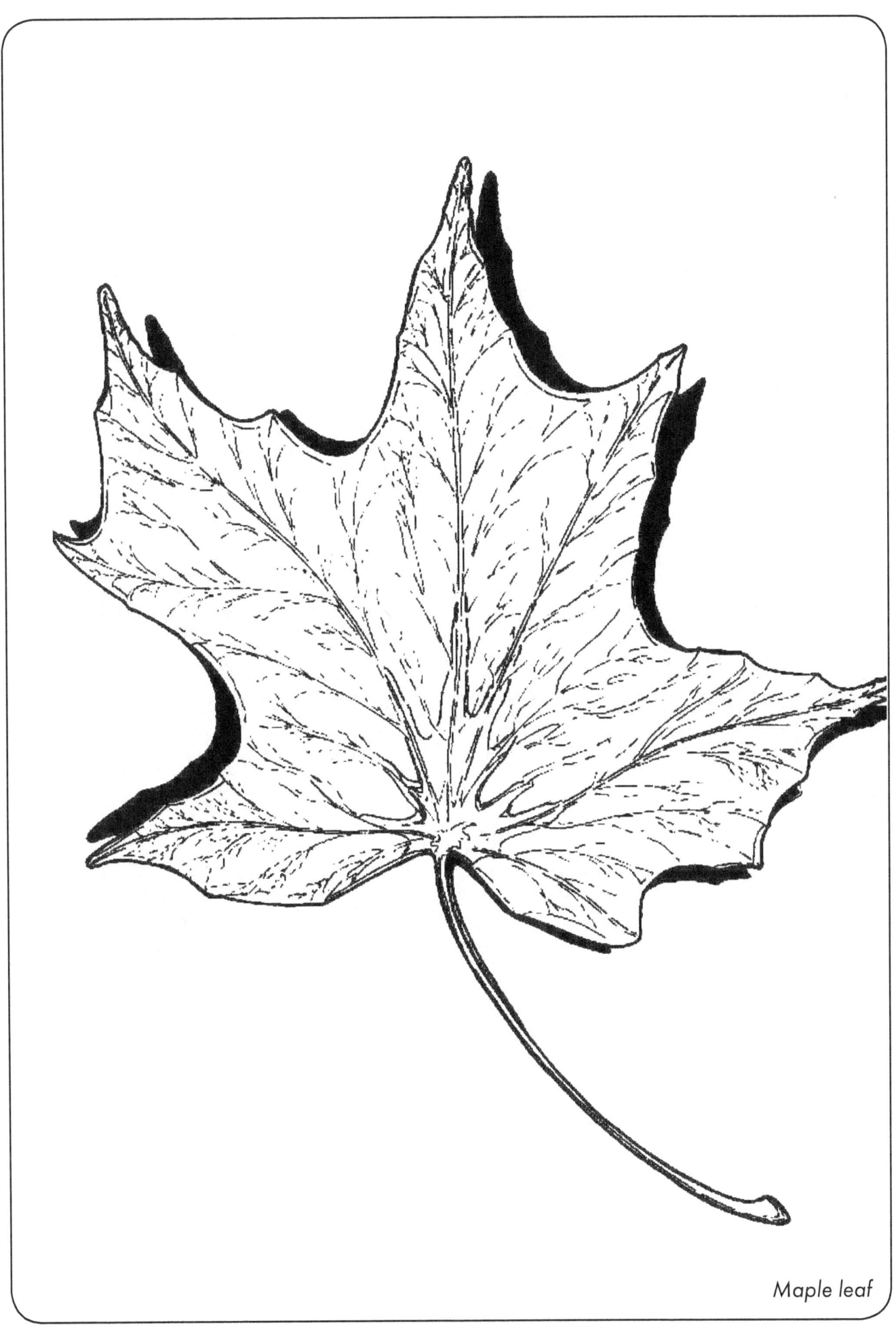

Maple leaf

Lilac

Lilacs are a flowering plant in the olive family.
The Americas were introduced to this flowering plant in the 18th century.
Several cities host a Lilac parade to celebrate this flower's beauty.
The city of Spokane, WA, started celebrating the Lilac in 1938
to showcase school marching bands and flower clubs.

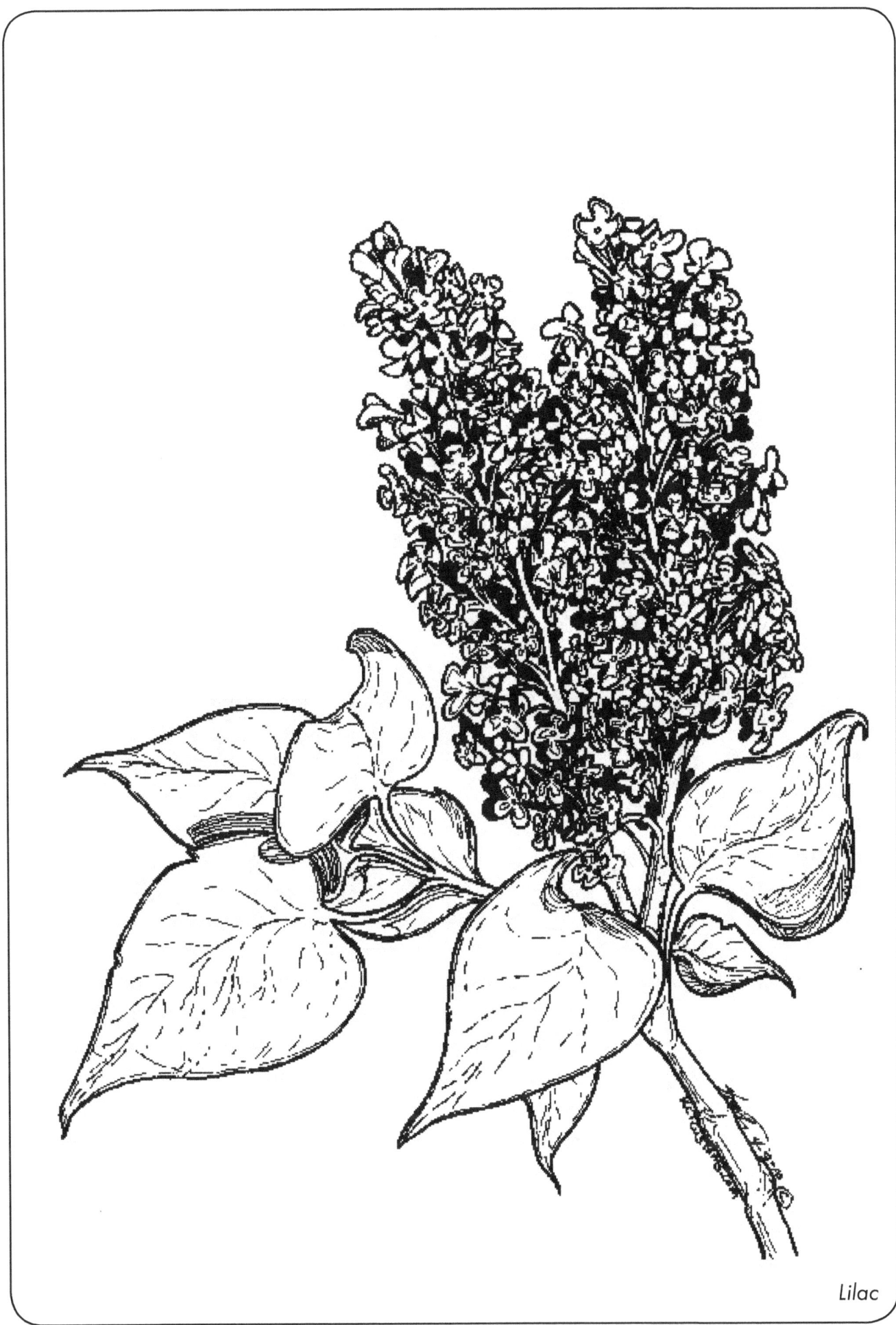

Lilac

Floral Sprig

St. Bernard's Lily is native to Europe and Turkey. It grows in wooded areas, rocky areas and dry pastures. These flowers produce six to ten white petals and blooms in the spring and summer.

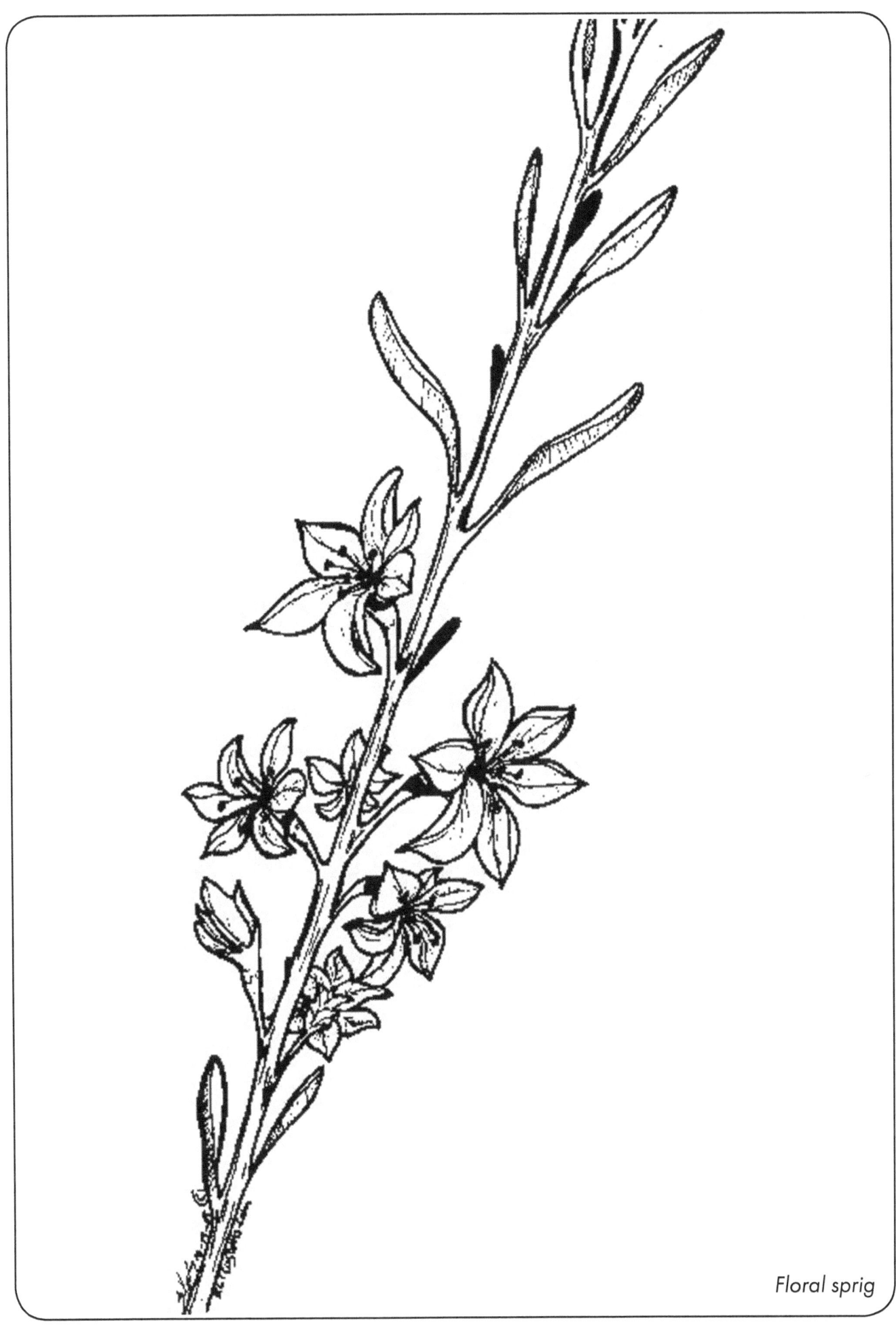

Floral sprig

Mango

Beautiful colors adorn the Mango's skin. These colors can range from greens to reds, oranges, and yellows. The actual fruit is an orange color and textures vary from soft and pulpy to firm like a cantaloupe.

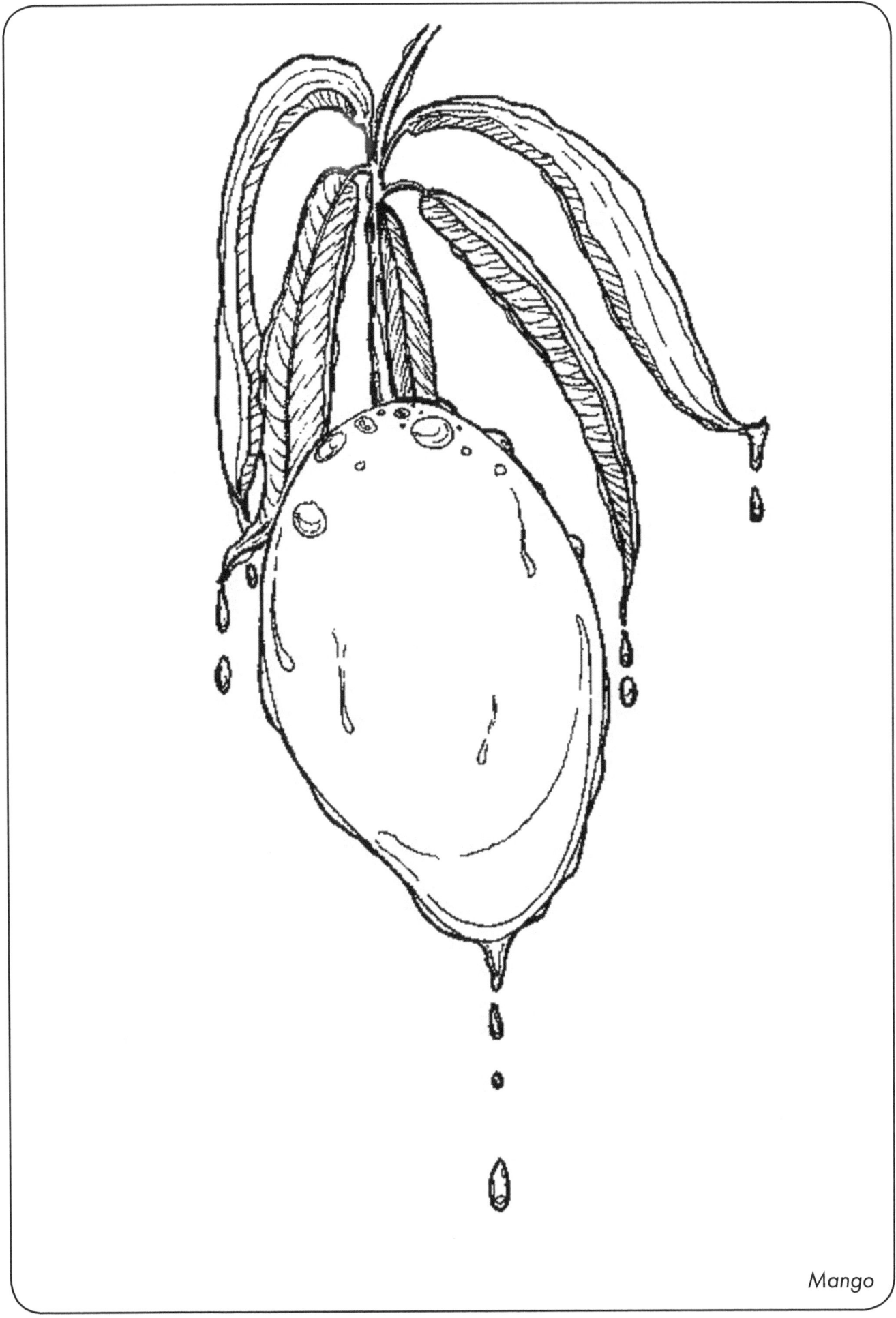

Mango

Rose

The Rose is a woody perennial flowering plant.
There are over 100 different species of roses.
Flower colors range from white to pink, red, yellow, and orange.

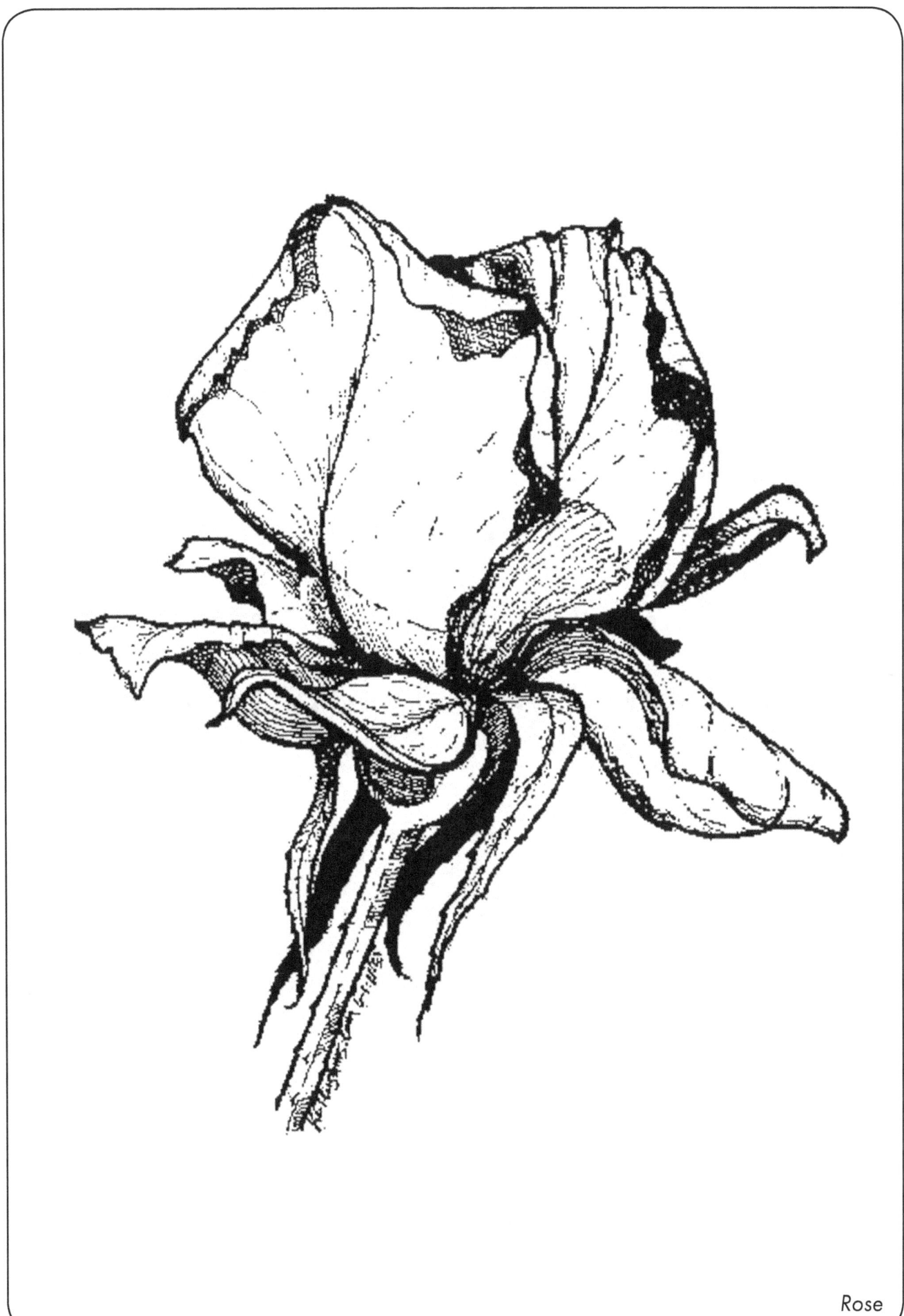

Rose

Iris

The African Iris is also called a Fortnight Lily and is native
to the southern part of Africa. They grow in dense clumps
and can grow from 18 to 24 inches tall and 9 to 12 inches wide.

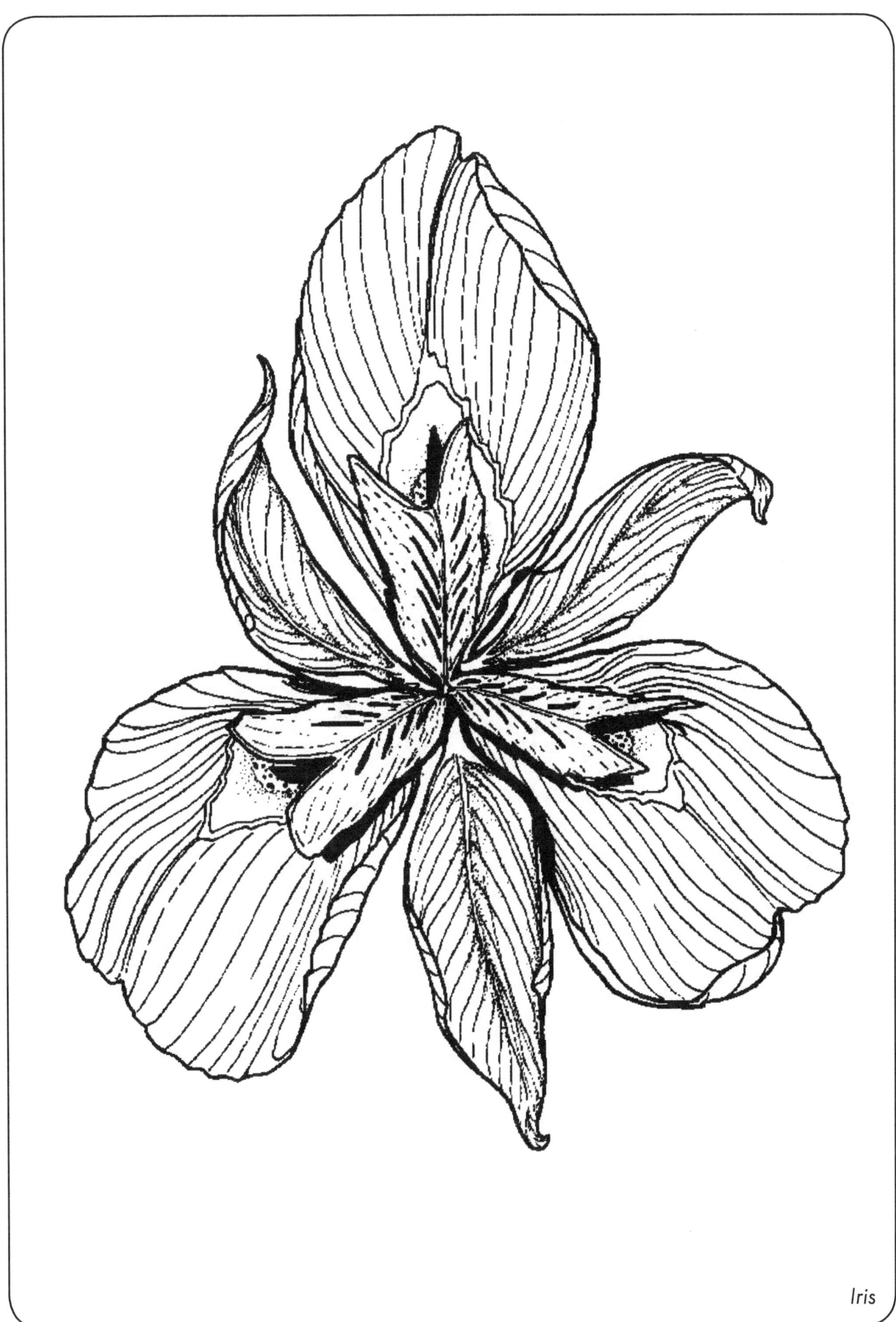

Iris

Iris

The Bearded Iris has a sweet fragrance that can fill a room.
This plant comes in many colors, with both solid and pattern varieties,
making it a favorite among growers.

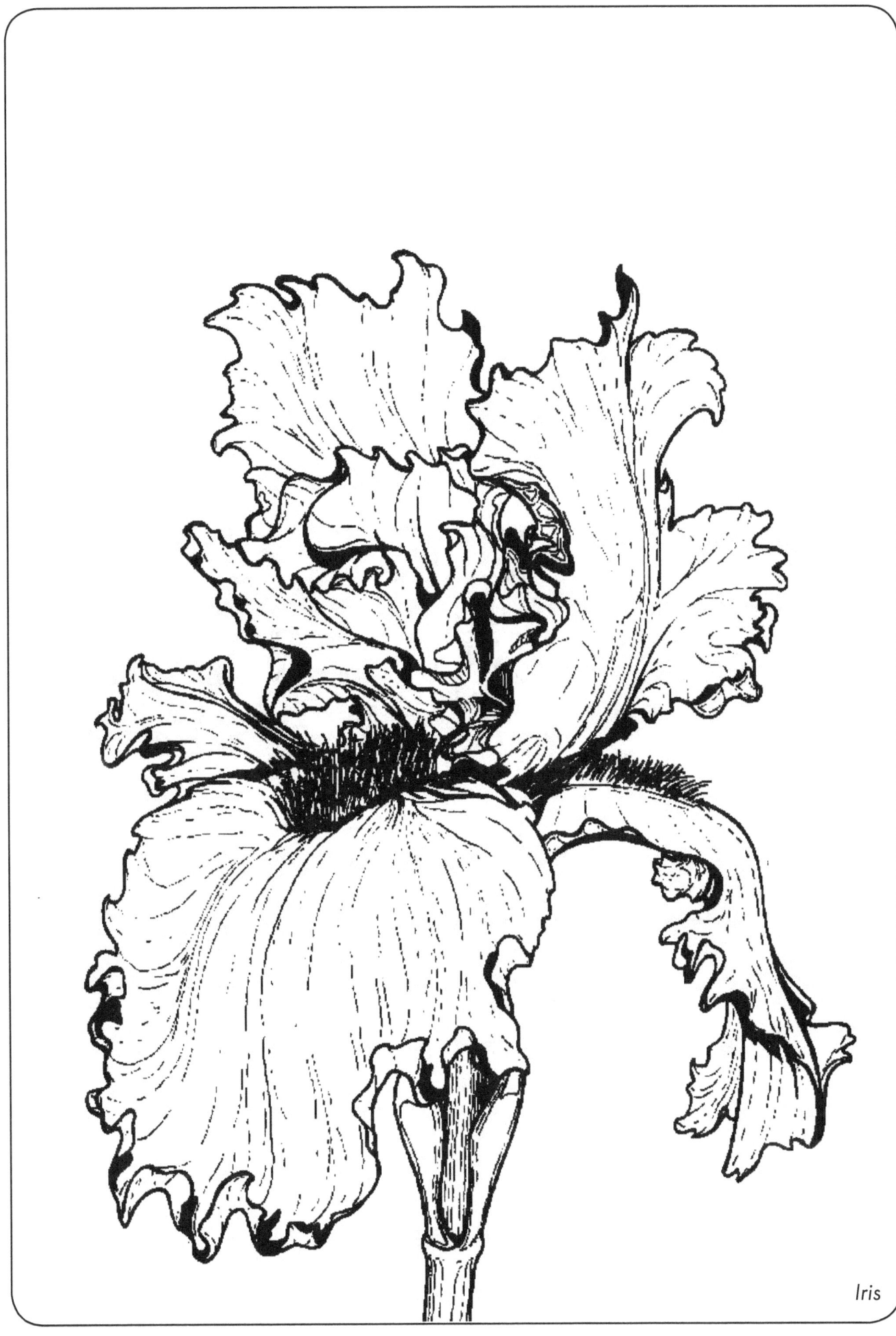

Iris

Lilies

The US Lilium started when a World War I soldier named Louis Houghton brought home a suitcase full of hybrid Lily bulbs.

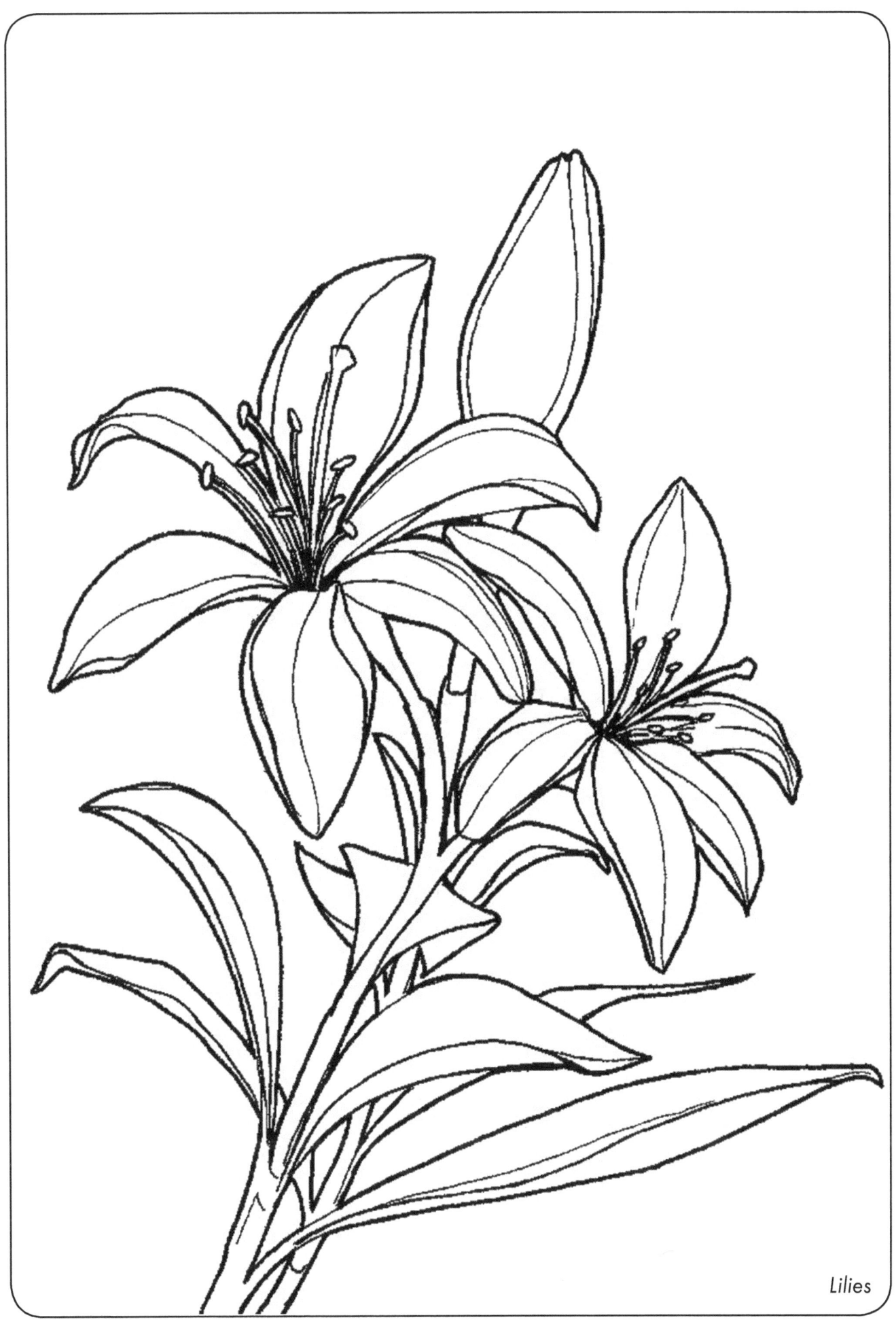

Lilies

Floral Display

Let your mind wander. Use your favorite shades and hues to color this collection
of different flowers. Reds, purples, blues, oranges, the choice is yours.
Combining several colors also works well.

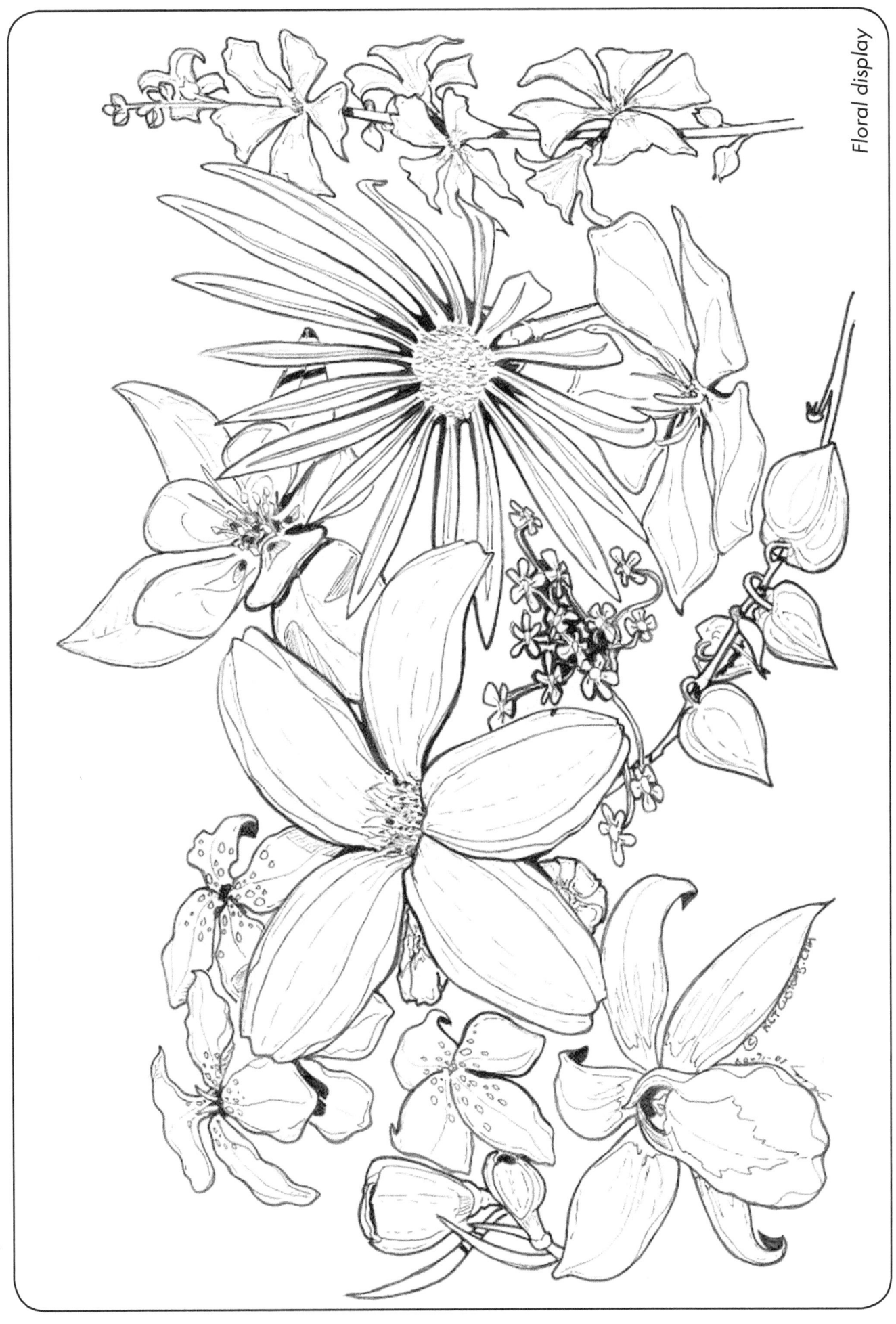

Lilies

Most lilies are grown for their beauty, smell, and ease of growth.
Some varieties are also grown for food! In China, Korea, and Japan,
three types of Lilies are cultivated for food — Lilium Brownii,
Lilium Pumilum, and Lilium Dauricum.

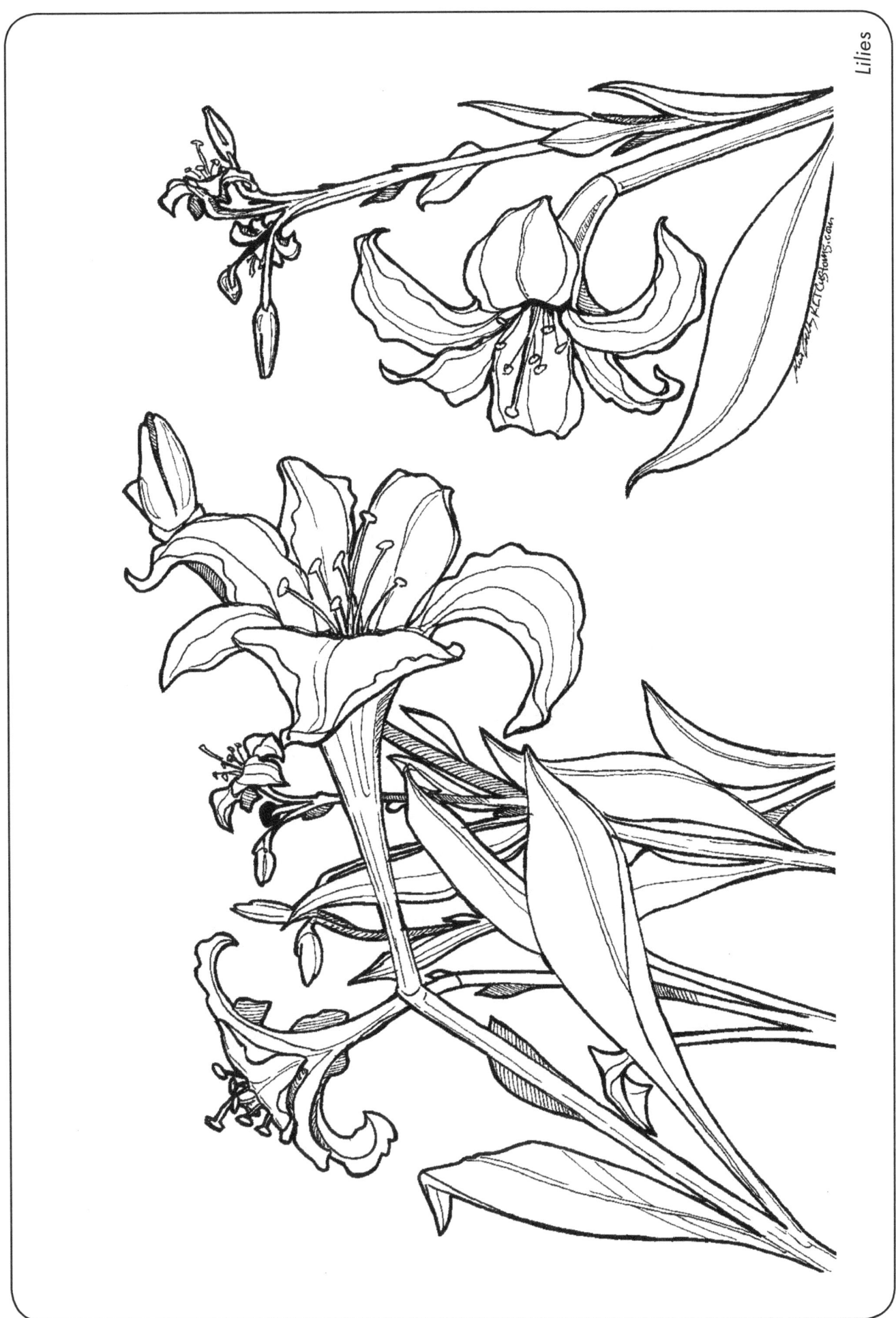

Peonies

The Peony are a flowering plant that is native to Asia, Europe and Western North America. The colors range from red, pink and white to brown at the end of May and June.

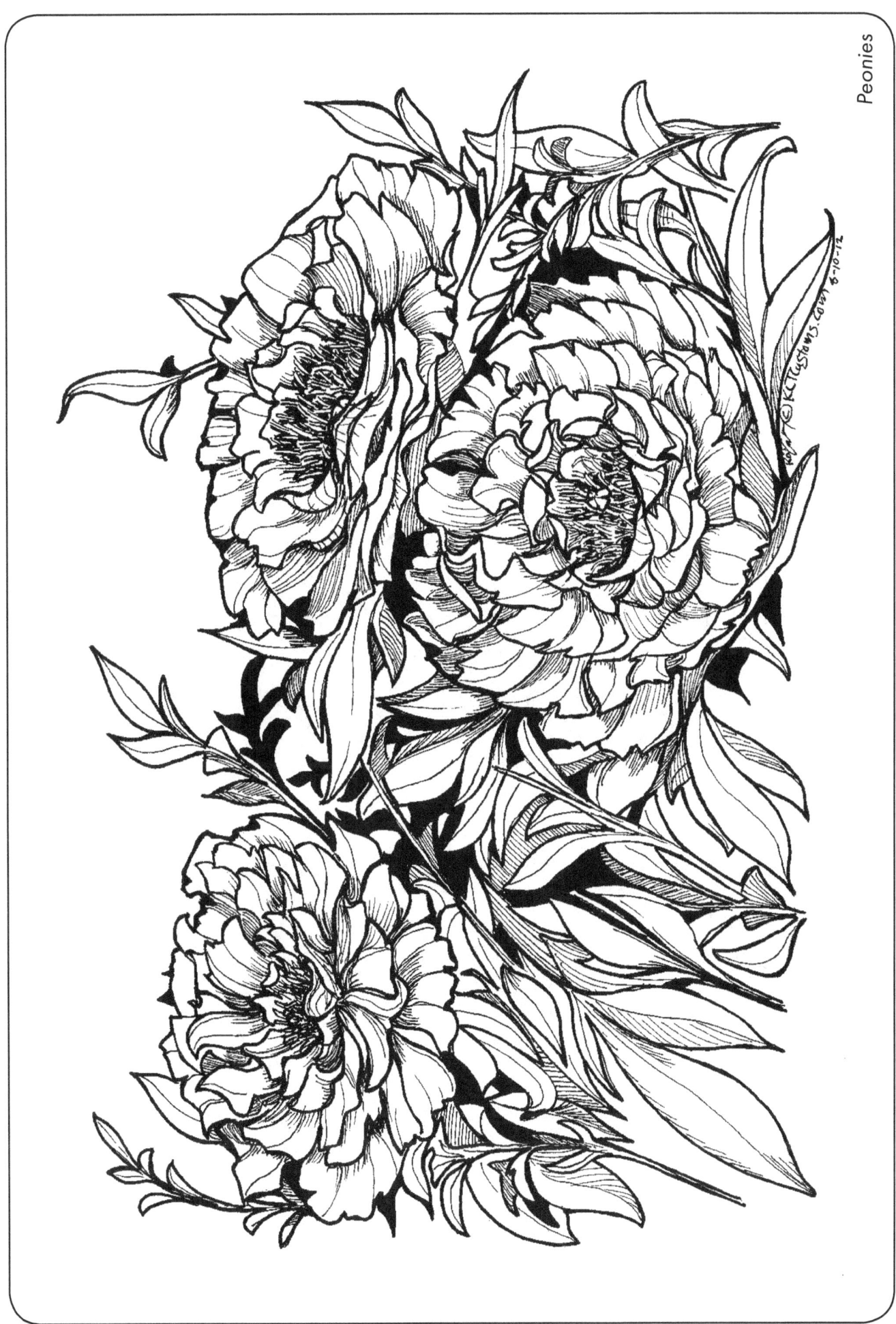

Gazania

The Gazania is in the Daisy family of plants. Often used as drought resistant ground cover in dry areas, this plant's flowerheads are daisy-like and have vibrant yellows and oranges.

8-10-12 KETCustoms.com

Lilies

Certain types of Lilies represent specific meanings in different parts of the world.

White Lilies represent purity and simplicity.

Day Lilies symbolize flirtation or romance.

Tiger Lilies are tied to wealth and royalty.

The Lily of the Valley is associated with family or loved ones.

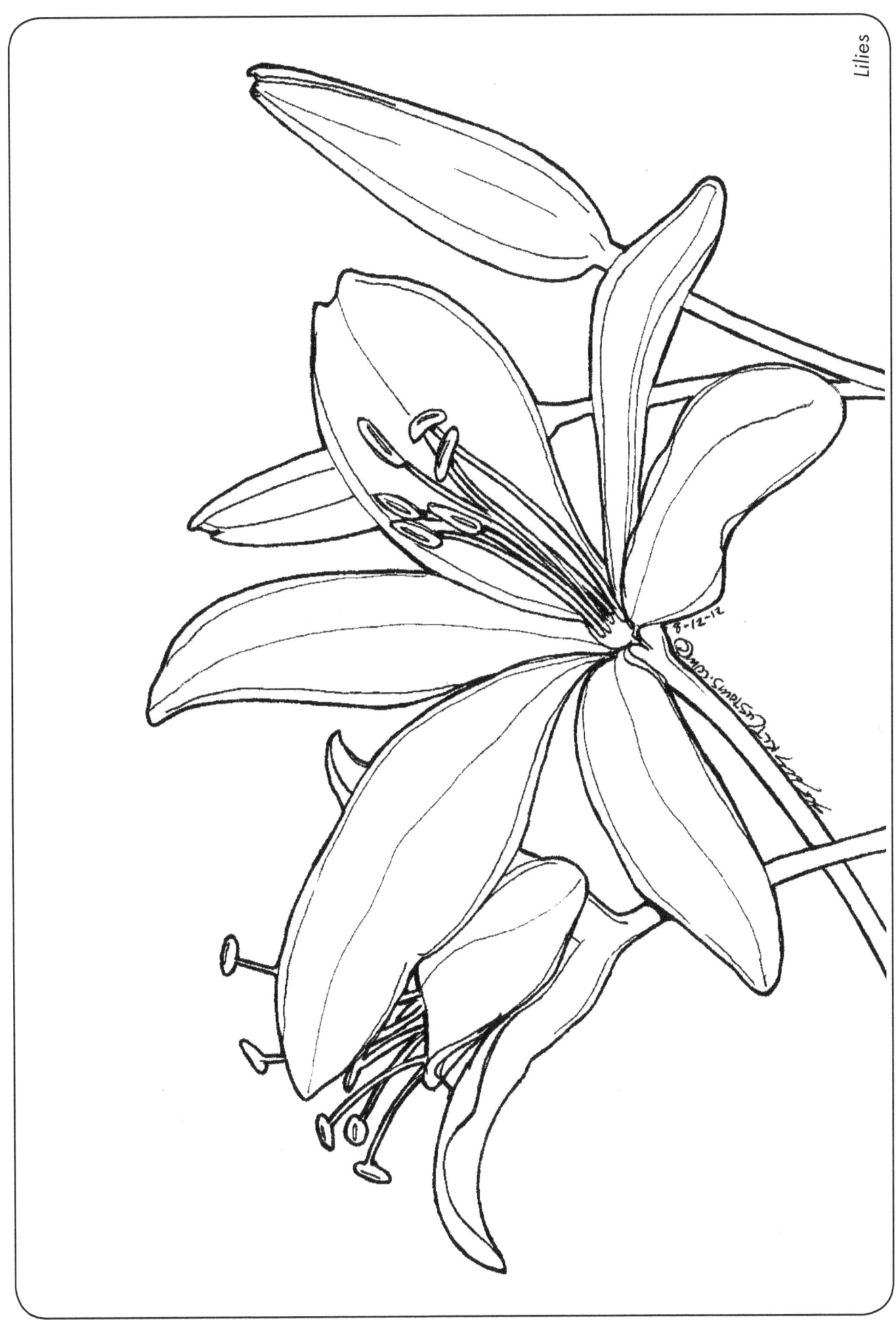

Gerbera Daisy

The Gerbera is another flowering plant in the Daisy family
and is native to the tropical regions of South America, Africa, and Asia.
Gerberas bloom in yellow, orange, white, pink and red.

8-12-12
KLCustoms.com

Amaryllis

The Amaryllis is also known as Belladona Lily, Jersey Lily, Naked Lily, and Amarillo. In Southern Australia, it is known as Eastern Lily. In South Africa it is called a March Lily because of the season in which it blooms.

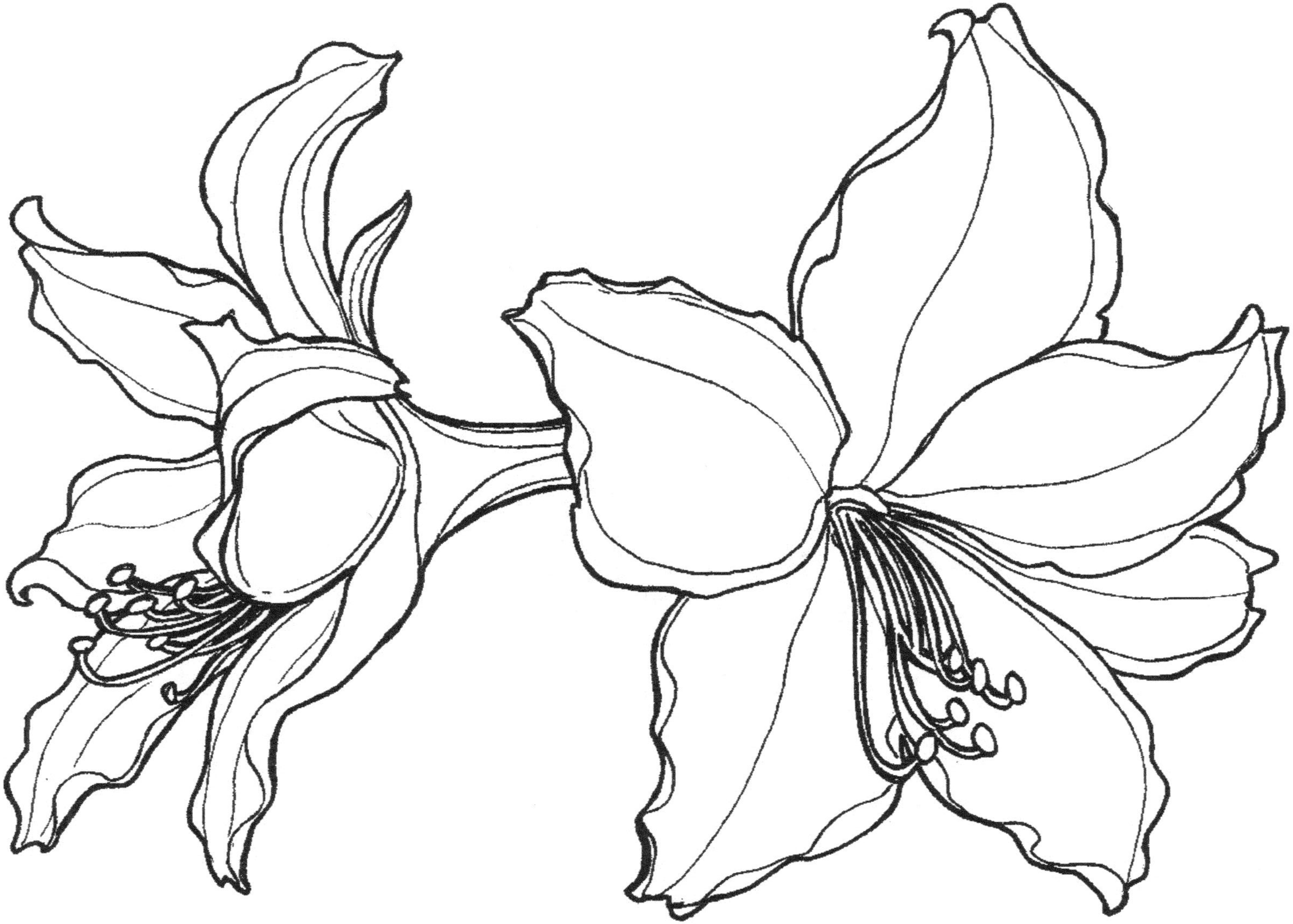

Amaryllis

Petunias

Petunia Flowers are from South America and are closely related to the Tobacco,
Cape Gooseberries, Tomato, Night Shade, Potato, and Chili Pepper plants.
The Incas and Mayan tribes believed that these flowers
would protect homes from evil spirits.

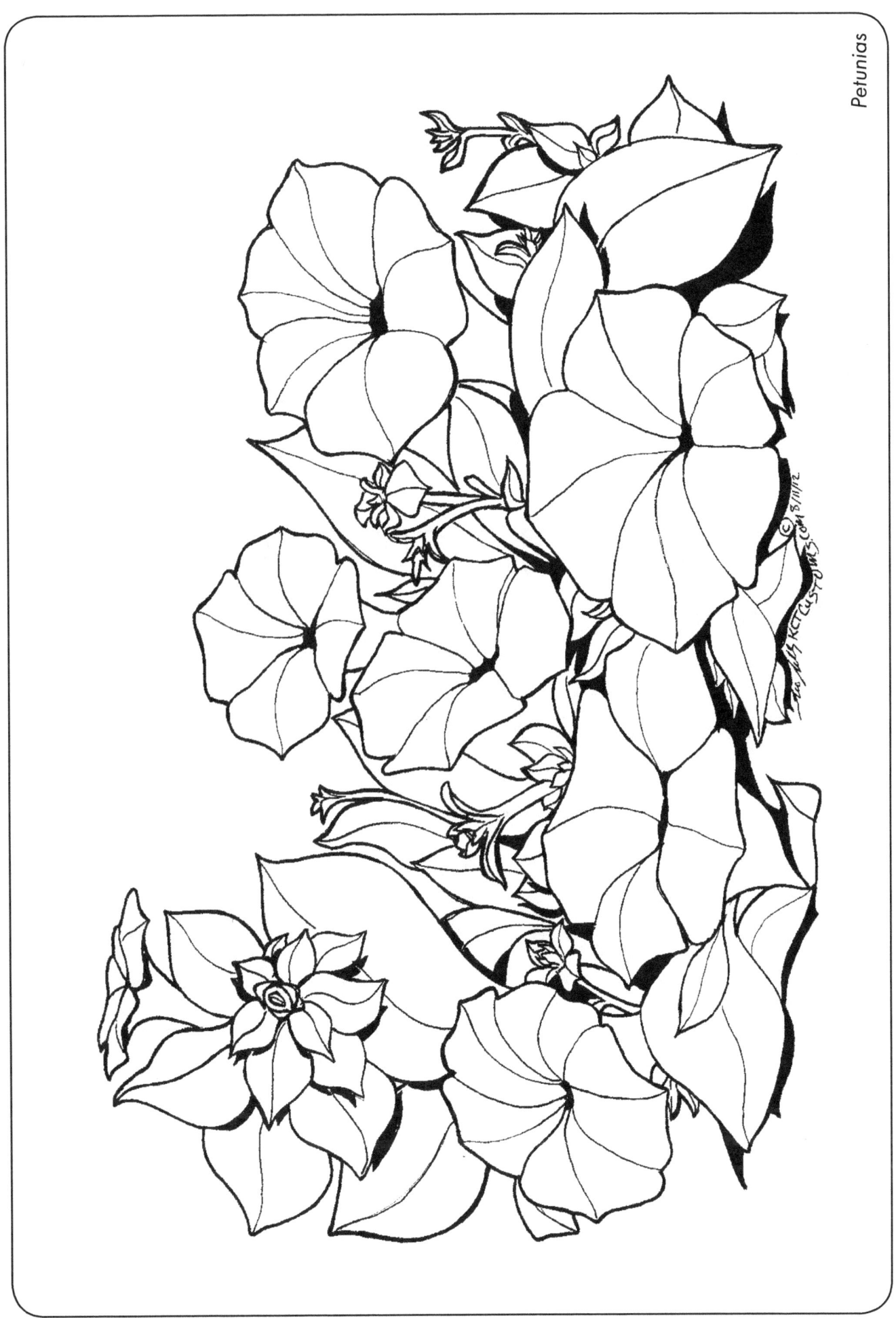

Star of Bethlehem

Star of Bethlehem is in the Lily family. It is native to the Mediterranean. The flower is small; about the size of your thumb, with a yellow center and white petals. The Star of Bethlehem blooms at night.

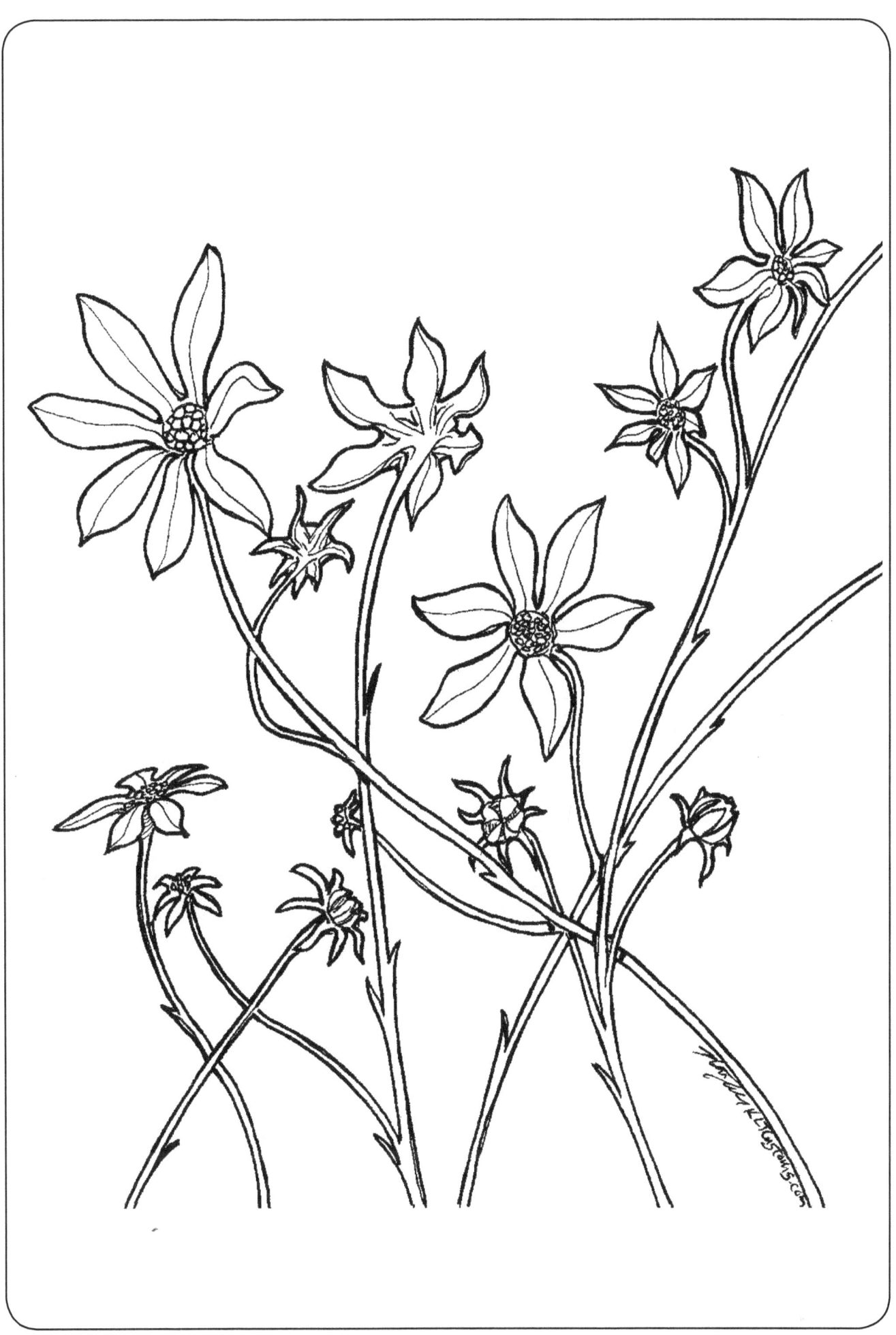

www.ingramcontent.com/pod-product-compliance
Lightning Source LLC
Chambersburg PA
CBHW080132240526
45468CB00009BA/2392